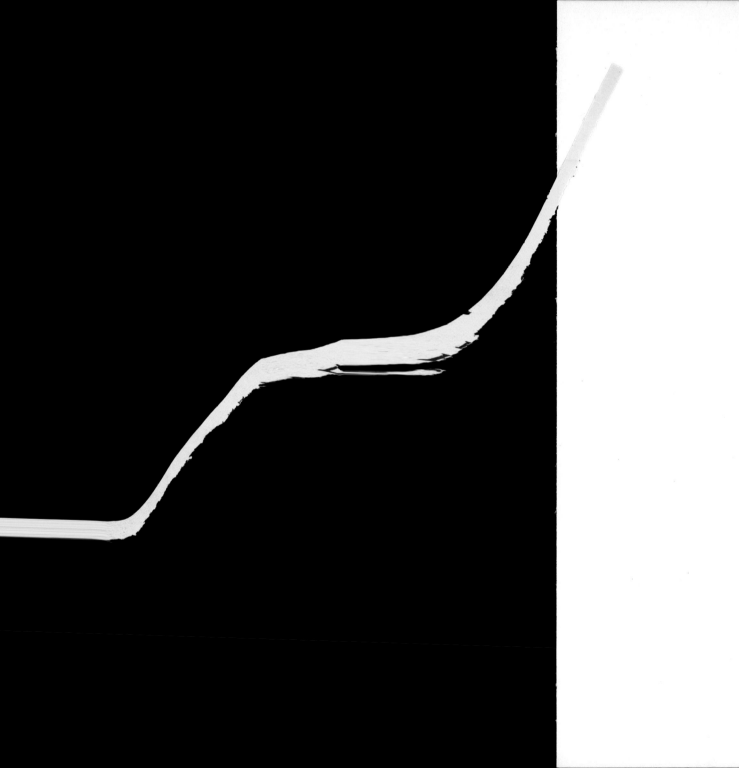

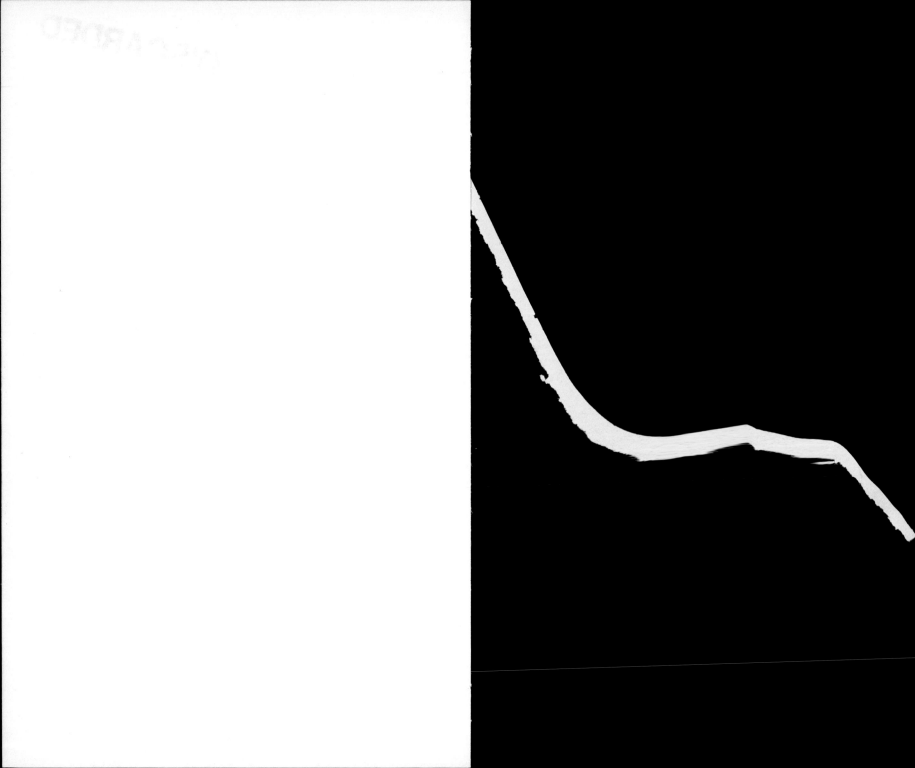

The Philosophical Roots of
Scientific Psychology

The Philosophical Roots of

Scientific Psychology

BY HENRYK MISIAK

Fordham University

FORDHAM UNIVERSITY PRESS • NEW YORK

Copyright © Fordham University Press 1961

LIBRARY OF CONGRESS CATALOG CARD NUMBER:
61-13026

ACKNOWLEDGMENTS

The author wishes to thank the following authors and publishers for their permission to reproduce quotations from their publications.

Persons:

Dr. Edwin G. Boring; Dr. Herbert Feigl; Rev. Edwin A. Quain, S. J.; Dr. Philip Wheelwright.

Publishers:

American Psychological Association for the quotation from *American Psychologist,* 1948, *3,* 548 (on p. 129-130);

Appleton-Century-Crofts, Inc. for the quotation from *A History of Experimental Psychology,* by Edwin G. Boring. Second edition copyright, 1950;

Fathers of the Church, Inc. for the excerpt from the translation of Tertullian's *De Anima* (on p. 20);

The Odyssey Press, Inc. for the excerpts from the translation of Aristotle's *De Anima* on pages 42 and 43;

The University of Minnesota Press for the quotation from *Concepts, Theories, and the Mind-Body Problem,* Volume II, Minnesota Studies in the Philosophy of Science, edited by Herbert Feigl, Michael Scriven, and Grover Maxwell, 1958 (on p. 62).

Contents

Preface

This book was not conceived with the intention of treating exhaustively the complete philosophical foundation of psychology. Rather, its purpose is practical, namely, to present the philosophical roots of scientific psychology in a simple manner and in concise form. It is addressed to students of psychology in colleges and graduate schools, particularly to those who have not had a broad training in philosophy. During some years of teaching psychology and the history of psychology, the author has found that students in general, and especially those without a background in philosophy, will encounter considerable difficulty in understanding the philosophical antecedents of psychological schools and theories. At the same time, it has been this author's conviction that such an understanding is essential in the study of the history of psychology.

It is for this reason that the book is offered and the following suggestions may well be helpful to students who may wish to go beyond the scope of the present book, to deepen their knowledge of the subject. The student will be wise, first, to endeavor to understand the philosophical doctrine itself, its proponents and their works and then to proceed to examine the effect of the doctrine on psychology. Obviously, the best way to study any doctrine or theory is to read the works in which it was originally expounded. If this be too much of a task for a student, he may profit much by reading pertinent excerpts from the great works. Valuable compilations of characteristic portions of our heritage of philosophical literature exist and some of them have been prepared with the student of psychology in mind. A list of these may be found at the end of the book.

Besides these works of the philosophers, the student will find much pleasure and enlightenment in such a work as the classic of psychological historiography, E.G. Boring's *A History of Experimental Psychology*. On particular topics, many books and articles are available. For the student who desires to delve more deeply into the subject, a list of supplementary readings is presented at the end of the book.

The author wishes to express his grateful thanks to Dr. Elizabeth G. Salmon, Associate Professor of Philosophy at Fordham University, for her reading of the manuscript and for all her helpful suggestions and corrections. All the inadequacies or errors, however, that may still remain in the book are the sole responsibility of the author.

Henryk Misiak

Introduction

In order to know and understand anything entirely, whether it be a country, a city, or a single event, one should also know its past. The same is true of a science. To know and understand a science, whether it be chemistry, biology, or psychology, it is not enough to be familiar with its present status, its data, laws, and methods. One has, as it were, to retrace its path to find how this science arrived at what it possesses now. Only then can he gain a true appreciation of it. Can we imagine a physicist unfamiliar with the work and contributions of Isaac Newton, or an astronomer unaware of the role of Copernicus and Kepler? Can a mathematician be ignorant of the beginnings of mathematics in the ancient world? Likewise, we expect that any physician would know the highlights of medical history.

There is a definite value in knowing the history of the science to which one intends to be dedicated. There are some who are so busy with experimental research and the collection of factual data that they may be tempted to consider the study of history a waste of time or a luxury to be avoided. Perhaps if they studied history they would find that the time spent on it paid handsome dividends in their research. The author recalls the late Professor Selig Hecht's frequent remarks in his lectures on sensory physiology at Columbia University concerning the profitable returns from the historical study of a research problem, and his denunciations of investigators who do not bother to acquaint themselves with the history of the problem which they intend to study. He himself always introduced a topic of sensory physiology with a historical review.

There is nothing to be lost, rather much to be gained, from an acquaintance with the historical past of any science. This is even more true of the history of psychology. For psychology studies man, his behavior and experience, and there is no subject more complex than that. By knowing how psychology approached the study of man, what difficulties it met and how it tried to overcome them, what successes and failures it had in the course of its development, one is bound to gain a deeper understanding and a better appreciation of its present status and of the prospects for its future development. Such knowledge will help one to see psychology in better perspective and to avoid errors committed in the past. It will lend encouragement to the student through the realization of psychology's successes and provoke a challenge through the presentation of its unsolved problems. The eminent historian of psychology, E. G. Boring, said in the introduction of his *A History of Experimental Psychology*:

The experimental psychologist, so it always seemed to me, needs historical sophistication within his own sphere of expertness. Without such knowledge he sees the present in distorted perspective, he mistakes old facts and old views for new, and he remains unable to evaluate the significance of new movements and methods. In this matter I can hardly state my faith too strongly. A psychological sophistication that contains no component of historical orientation seems to me to be no sophistication at all.

The Philosophical Roots of
Scientific Psychology

1

Genealogy of Psychology

WHAT IS PRESENT DEPENDS MUCH UPON WHAT REMAINS BEHIND.
Francis Bacon

There is Always a Past.

Everything that exists today had its antecedents in the past, often, a long-ago yesterday. There is nothing in nature or in the sphere of human life without a long chain of events preceding it. A hen comes from an egg, a tree from a seed, and their growth and characteristics are determined by the potentialities which existed in the egg or the seed. Similarly, in the history of mankind, even human discoveries or inventions which appear to be fortuitous or sudden, can occur, as we learn in the history of culture, only if certain events have preceded them or if certain favorable conditions have existed. The discovery of America by Columbus could not have been possible in 1492 if, in addition to his decision and ability, there were no ocean-going ships, knowledge of navigation, financial support, notion of the curvature of the earth, desire to reach India, and other things. If we turn to the origin and growth of the sciences we find that each of them was preceded by a long series of events and a slow accumulation of various observations and facts. As R. S. Peters said in his revision of *Brett's History of Psychology*, "... no one starts afresh in the acquisition of knowledge. We all stand on the shoulders of our ancestors ..."

1

Man's Desire to Know.

The ultimate reason for the origin of the sciences, of course, was the inquisitive mind of man. Man wanted to know his surroundings, the forces of nature, and himself. As both Plato and Aristotle said, philosophy begins in wonder. One of the most amazing characteristics of the human mind is its relentless desire to know, to learn, and to discover, even if there are no immediate practical returns or gains, in fact, even at considerable pain and sacrifice. Practical application of man's knowledge usually came much later, often unexpectedly or unintentionally. The history of astronomy, biology, or physics bears out this fact.

The Origin of Psychology in Philosophy.

Psychology, like all sciences, also had its ultimate source in that basic and powerful drive for knowledge and in man's curiosity about the world and himself. It emerged from inquiries into and speculations about the nature of man. Such inquiries and speculations were attempted by men interested in medicine, religion, and philosophy. Since in its inquiries philosophy, which in literal definition is "the love of wisdom," endeavored to encompass all points of view, it is in its womb that psychology was conceived, as were all other sciences. The very beginnings of this oldest branch of human knowledge were also therefore the beginnings of psychology. Psychology as an independent science, however—that is, *scientific psychology*, defined now as the science of behavior and experience, distinct from philosophy or its special branch, philosophical psychology, traces its origin from the middle of the nineteenth century.

The Province of Philosophy

We suppose that we should, at the outset of our inquiry into

2

the philosophical roots of psychology, delineate, if only briefly, the province of philosophy with respect to the study of man. Both philosophy and psychology study man, but each from a different angle and by different methods. Psychology studies man's behavior, understood in a broad sense, including overt behavior as well as any covert activity like feeling, perceiving, thinking, by means of scientific methods. The objective of psychology is to describe this behavior, measure it, explain it on the basis of scientific data, and predict it whenever possible. Thus, psychology occupies a position between the social and biological sciences with some of its branches belonging definitely to social and others clearly to biological sciences.

Although the philosophy of man begins with observation of man's basic activities, it seeks through reflection upon them to determine man's nature and ultimately his relation to all beings. It is the essential and the ultimate of the human nature that philosophy seeks to determine. Hence the philosophical viewpoint with respect to man's nature is thus more general and broader than the psychological one. Psychology and philosophy represent two levels of knowledge of the same subject and therefore can be considered complementary to each other. More allusions to the psychology-philosophy relationship will be made later in the book, but the student interested in this problem, which deserves more extensive treatment than we can give here, is referred to special books. During the long gestation of psychology, which lasted for about 24 centuries, psychology was part of philosophy without having its own differentiated identity. It was only in the nineteenth century that psychology ceased to be philosophical and became scientific. The account of the gestation of psychology within philosophy and of the effect which that long association with philosophy had on psychology constitutes the contents of this book.

Emancipation of Psychology from Philosophy

There were many varied factors in the emancipation of psychology from philosophy in the nineteenth century. These factors can be referred, on one hand, to the realization of the incompleteness and inadequacy of solely philosophical treatment of psychological problems, and on the other hand, to the progress and findings of physiology which contained elements of psychological significance.

In the nineteenth century men interested in psychology began to realize that philosophy alone, since it stemmed from intellectual reflection on man's activities, could only achieve an understanding of the general principles of man's nature. Because of its subject matter and methods, philosophy was found incapable of solving satisfactorily, from the scientific point of view, the various psychological problems which had been posed in the past and which recurred with urgency demanding investigation and solutions. It was then realized that philosophy could not provide satisfactory answers, for instance, to all the questions pertaining to sensation, perception, learning, emotions, and similar processes. In the light of scientific progress particularly, it became apparent that psychological problems, traditionally treated by philosophy, now required, in order to be in step with this progress, a new treatment and a different approach. Moreover, new problems arose such as hypnotism, reaction time, mental abnormalities, which were expected to be studied by psychology and which obviously were beyond the province of philosophy.

The inadequacy of exclusive philosophical treatment of psychological problems came into even sharper focus when discoveries in neuroanatomy and physiology provided much material of psychological relevance and when physiologists' explanations were often more satisfactory and convincing than those of philosophers. Furthermore, certain experiments performed by physiologists shed new light on the human mind and called for revision of some notions about man handed down by philosophy. Such experiments demonstrated at the same time that the human mind could be studied not only in the philosopher's armchair but also in the laboratory, and with results which could be subjected to scientific verification. Consequently, those interested in the psychological study of man began to feel the need of experimentation and of studying also the biological aspects of man, and of knowing the nervous system, the function of the brain, and other physiological functions. Mathematics likewise came to be valued as a useful discipline in psychological inquiries whenever they aimed not merely at description but quantitative analysis.

The conclusion from the above suggested itself forcefully: psychology could no longer remain a mere chapter of philosophy; it should seek contact with other sciences, incorporate pertinent findings of these sciences, particularly of physiology, develop its own methods, and institute a new inquiry of man. Subsequent chapters will present in greater detail the developments which led to this conclusion.

The Birth of Scientific Psychology in the Nineteenth Century.

In the light of the above discussion, it is apparent that the separation of psychology from philosophy was a logical and inevitable consequence. It occurred in the 1870's, and during this decade, and in subsequent years, many writers reflected the birth of the new science in various ways: definitions of the new psychology were proposed, objectives and methods were formulated, textbooks and treatises were written. But the most important single event signaling the new science was the establishment of the first psychological laboratory. This particular event has been regarded by historians as the formal beginning of scientific psychology because it was a clear sign of the latter's departure from philosophical methods and the turning to experimentation. This first laboratory was opened in 1878, but since the first experimetal study was completed in 1879, this year has been acclaimed the birthyear of psychology. This first laboratory, which was to remain for a few decades the most important place of research and training and a model for other laboratories, was opened at the University of Leipzig in Germany, due to the influence and under the direction of *Wilhelm Wundt* (1832-1920), professor of philosophy at that university. Wundt has been hailed as the originator of scientific psychology and has been called the father of psychology, and his laboratory, the cradle of experimental research in psychology.

Continued Influence of Philosophy on Psychology.

Thus psychology, separated from philosophy, started an independent existence as a new, autonomous, experimental science. All other major scientific disciplines such as astronomy, biology, and physics were also once part of philosophy but they separated from it much earlier than psychology. That is why psychology has been called the youngest of all sciences, and that is why Hermann Ebbinghaus (1850-1909), one of the builders of the new psychology, said that psychology had a long past (associated with philosophy) but a short history (as an independent science). Despite its emancipation, however, psychology stayed close to philosophy and continued to be influenced by it. The language of philosophy and the philosophical notions about man and his mental functions were still part of psychology, and the various philosophical systems continued to exert a strong influence on psychology and its development. Numerous psychologists, for many years, used philosophical doctrines or certain philosophical notions as their starting points and frames of reference.

6

The Role of Other Sciences in the Birth of Psychology.

The emancipation of psychology was due chiefly to the science of physiology which, particularly from the mid-nineteenth century, developed rapidly and made one discovery after another. Some of its discoveries such as those in the anatomy and functions of the nervous system, of the brain in particular, and in the sense organs had a direct bearing on psychological problems. There were, nonetheless, other influences which contributed to this emancipation of psychology: the interest and studies in the phenomena of hypnotism and suggestion, the discovery of reaction time, and the theory of evolution. Any finding pertaining to man, his nature, behavior, and position in human society inevitably affected the growth of psychology. Biological theories, ethnological and anthropological studies, the rise of the new science of genetics, interest in education, sociology and animal studies, all in greater or lesser degree had something to do with the origin and growth of the science of psychology.

Physiology as a Parent of Psychology.

As we stated above, nineteenth century physiology was the most important factor in the emancipation of psychology. The influence of physiology was evident and readily recognized by the pioneers of psychology many of whom were originally physiologists. The two greatest pioneers, Wilhelm Wundt in Germany and William James in America, both had medical degrees, and both taught physiology before they turned to psychology. The new psychology was named *physiological* psychology and its first textbook in Europe was entitled *Grundzüge der physiologischen Psychologie* or in English translation *Principles of Physiological Psychology* (W. Wundt), published in 1873-4 while the first published in America in 1887 was *Elements of Physiological Psychology* (G. T. Ladd). The first

7

International Congress of the new science in 1889 was called the Congress of *Physiological* Psychology.

The present meaning of physiological psychology is not the same as it was then. Currently, physiological psychology refers to the special branch of psychology which studies the physiological correlates of psychological processes and behavior. In the latter part of the nineteenth century, however, physiological psychology denoted not just a part, but the whole new science. The adjective *physiological* seemed at that time the most appropriate title for a number of reasons. Primarily because it was the progress of physiology which in several ways spurted the development of psychology and led to its emancipation. Moreover, a large segment of the early psychology, practically all sensory psychology, was assimilated directly from physiology. Various other fields of psychology similarly profited from the contributions of physiologists. The experimental methods used so effectively by physiologists, especially in the study of sensation, were also adopted by the new psychology. The dependence of psychology on physiology and the intimate relationship between psychology and physiology were reflected in the widely approved statement made by the outstanding physiologist of the time, Johannes Müller, that *nemo psychologus nisi physiologus* ("no one can be a psychologist unless he is a physiologist").

A characteristic passage from the first American textbook of physiological psychology, Ladd's *Elements of Physiological Psychology,* 1887. p. 10.

The history of modern investigation, and the conclusions of the modern science of man, both physical and psychological, emphasize the necessity of studying his nature and development as that of a living unity. Such science shows man to be at the head of a series of physical and psychical existences; he cannot be understood as he is, in his whole nature and in his place within nature at large, without taking both sides of this living unity into account. For man is known to himself as body *and* mind—and not as bodiless spirit or a mindless congeries of moving molecules. That the structure and functions of the body, especially of the nervous mechanism, and the activities of the mind, are extensively and intimately correlated, is a fact beyond all doubt. It is the particular task of Physiological Psychology to show in what manner, and to what extent, such correlation exists. Moreover, there are few questions more interesting, from a philosophical and an ethical point of view, than such as the following: What is the nature of mind, considered in the light of its correlations with the body? and, Do the so-called physiological and the so-called psychical phenomena belong to one subject, or to more than one? But these and similar questions can be scientifically answered only by giving a speculative treatment to the conclusions of psycho-physical investigation.

In brief, it may be said that introspective psychology, important as its results have been, and indispensable as its method is, has shown its incompetency to deal with many of the most interesting inquiries which it has itself raised. On the other hand, psychology as pursued by the experimental and physiological method has already thrown a flood of fresh light upon many of these inquiries. We may affirm with Wundt, without fear of successful contradiction: "Psychology is compelled to make use of objective changes in order, by means of the influences which they exert on our consciousness, to establish the subjective properties and laws of that consciousness." On this fact and on the real achievements of the method we confidently rest its claims to serious and permanent consideration.

Among the physiologists of the ninteenth century, the three who directly and importantly influenced psychology were E. H. Weber, J. Müller, and H. Helmholtz. *Ernst Heinrich Weber* (1795-1878) contributed to psychology by his research on the sense of touch, by his methods of measuring sensitivity, and by his findings with respect to the relationship between stimulus and sensation (Weber's law). *Johannes Müller* (1801-1858), called the "father of experimental physiology," gave prominence to psychological matters in his encyclopedic *Handbook of Physiology* (1834-1840) and formulated the theory of

9

specific energies of nerves, which stimulated much research on sensation. *Hermann von Helmholtz* (1821-1894) was particularly esteemed by psychologists for his studies of vision and hearing, and being regarded almost as one of their own, was invited to psychological congresses in which he willingly participated.

Contribution of New Methodology to Psychology.

Besides its philosophical and physiological parentage psychology received considerable assistance from a new scientific methodology which was developed by other sciences in the second half of the nineteenth century and which was found highly suitable for psychological investigations. This new methodology contributed substantially to psychology's weaning from philosophy and its acquisition of scientific status.

Any science in order to exist and advance must have its own methods. Proper methods, tools, and procedures are often critical in the pursuit of science's objectives and its achievements. Quite often, as the history of science demonstrates, the invention or adoption of a new method or instrument constituted a decisive factor in the progress of a given science. The progress of many branches of science frequently waited on the development of suitable methods and tools, and was accelerated as soon as some new method or instrument was discovered. Astronomy's progress was hastened by the invention of the telescope and other optical instruments. Biology could make rapid advances when the microscope was invented, and the cathode-ray made possible the invention of radio, television and the like. Similar examples could be multiplied from different sciences. Psychology needed its own methods too. In order to assert its independence from philosophy, to rise to the level of a science, and to assure its growth, it had to find methods and procedures, which while suited to its subject-matter, would also comply with the criteria of modern science. It found them first in the system of psychophysics.

Psychophysics.

Psychophysics furnished psychology with the first useful methods. With its new, promising for psychology, concepts it also became a powerful stimulus and inspiration for psychological research. Psychophysics was founded in Leipzig, the birthplace of psychology, by *Gustav Theodor Fechner* (1801-1887) who introduced it in 1860 in his book *The Elements of Psychophysics,* a book which some hailed as the actual beginning of scientific psychology. Fechner intended psychophysics to be much more than a mere methodology. It was, according to his definition, "an exact science of the functional relation or relations of dependency between body and mind." However, it was primarily the methodology and not the philosophy of psychophysics which the new psychology seized upon, applied, and subsequently further developed.

In modern definition, psychophysics is "that branch of psychology which deals with measurement in the subjective or experiential continuum" (L. L. Thurstone). Its chief object has been to find what the minimum magnitude of the physical stimulus must be to be perceived by the subject at all (absolute threshold), and how far two stimuli must be apart to be noticed as different (differential threshold), a study which greatly occupied first psychologists. Special methods used in this study are known as the psychophysical methods whose first systematic presentation was the work of Fechner in 1860.

Diagrammatic Presentation of the Genealogy of Psychology.

The understanding of the genealogy of psychology entails the study of the philosophical systems from which psychology emerged, of physiology, and of the scientific methodology adopted by psychology. Philosophy was the primary root of psychology because it was in philosophy that psychological thought originated, developed, and grew. It was also philosophy which was responsible for the general character and subject matter of the early psychology. Terminology, concepts, and theoretical framework came from philosophy too. It was, however, physiology which was the main factor in psychology's emancipation and which spurred its independent development along new scientific lines. That is why physiology is considered the second root of psychology. And the third root, scientific methodology, incorporated by psychology, contributed to psychology's experimental and quantitative character and thus also to its growth as a science.

We can summarize all that we have said about the genealogy of scientific psychology in the diagram which follows. In it we specify the philosophical, physiological, and methodological parentage of psychology, and we also indicate the other sources which contributed to the growing psychology. The three main streams of influence, the philosophical, physiological, and methodological, converged, so to speak, in Wilhelm Wundt who was at once a physiologist, a philosopher, and a psychophysicist. Well trained in all these three fields, he was well prepared for his role as father of scientific psychology.

SUMMARY

Scientific psychology originated in the last quarter of the nineteenth century. Its origin was prepared by philosophy and science. The most important root of psychology was philosophy. The others were physiology and scientific methodology. The philosophical past played a significant role in shaping psychology's character and development. Psychology began its existence as a separate science when it broke away from philosophy, in the 1870's.

THE PARENTAGE OF SCIENTIFIC PSYCHOLOGY AND THE MAIN SOURCES OF INFLUENCE ON ITS GROWTH

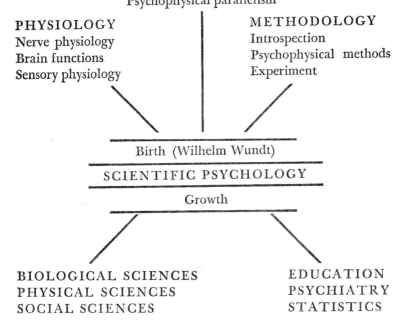

PHILOSOPHY
Empirical philosophy
Associationism
Psychophysical parallelism

PHYSIOLOGY
Nerve physiology
Brain functions
Sensory physiology

METHODOLOGY
Introspection
Psychophysical methods
Experiment

Birth (Wilhelm Wundt)

SCIENTIFIC PSYCHOLOGY

Growth

BIOLOGICAL SCIENCES
PHYSICAL SCIENCES
SOCIAL SCIENCES

EDUCATION
PSYCHIATRY
STATISTICS

13

2

Psychology Within Philosophy

All of the preceding discussion was intended to give a general idea about the origin of scientific psychology. Now we can concentrate exclusively on the philosophical roots of psychology. It will be perhaps helpful if we explain at this point what we mean by "philosophical roots."

What is Meant by "Philosophical Roots"?

The philosophical roots of psychology—in our understanding—comprise all the labors and ideas of philosophers which resulted in the gradual development of psychology and produced that psychology which we find at the time of its emancipation from philosophy. In other words, by philosophical roots we mean all the philosophical past which was responsible and accounted for the new psychology at the end of the nineteenth century. Our thesis is that this new psychology reflects its philosophical heritage in the following respects:

 a) definition and subject-matter,
 b) fundamental concepts and terminology,
 c) main topic of study (consciousness),
 d) chief method (introspection),
 e) basic characteristics,
 f) general orientation.

14

The purpose of this book is to show this effect of philosophy on psychology, in a concise and simple manner, for the benefit of the psychology student. To achieve this purpose, we need not study the entire history of philosophy. It will suffice to point out only the milestones of psychological thought in philosophy, particularly those philosophical schools or those concepts which actually affected scientific psychology.

Plan of Our Discussion

We divide the analysis of the philosophical roots into two parts. The first part will outline the growth of psychological thought in philosophy in a historical sequence, from antiquity up to Descartes, that is, to the beginning of modern philosophy in the seventeenth century. That long period comprises developments which we can call the remote or distant roots. The second part will concentrate on the immediate roots, that is, on those philosophical doctrines which were closely related to the new psychology and were directly responsible for its origin, characteristics, and orientation. Some overlapping of material in the discussion of these two phases will be unavoidable. The first phase will be the subject of this chapter, whereas the second will be discussed in the subsequent chapters.

It will be appropriate to commence the discussion with the explanation of the meaning of the word *psychology* and *psychological thought.*

The Term "Psychology."

The word "psychology," like many scientific terms, comes from Greek. It is composed of two words, *psyche*—the soul or mind, and *logos*—knowledge or study. Literally, it means the study, knowledge, or science of the soul. And that is what psychology was when the word was coined. It is Philip Melanchthon (1497-1560), the collaborator of Martin Luther,

15

who is credited with this coinage. But the term came into general usage only about a hundred years later. Christian von Wolff (1679-1754) popularized it when he distinguished between *empirical* and *rational* psychology, and wrote separate treatises on each of them (1732, 1734).

There were also other names for this science in simultaneous use, in the eighteenth and nineteenth centuries. Mental philosophy, autology (science of one's self), and pneumatology (science of spirits or "created intelligences") are some of them. The definitions and topics of psychology, regardless of the name it bore, differed widely.

Development of Psychological Thought

Under the name *psychological thought* we understand the treatment of all the problems pertaining to human nature, to soul and mind, consciousness, mental processes and activities such as sensation, perception, learning, cognition, reasoning, feeling, and volition. These topics were studied until the nineteenth century chiefly by various philosophers in different ways with conclusions differing from one system to another. We encounter interest in some of these subjects at the dawn of human thought and we see ever increasing and widening study of psychological problems throughout ancient philosophy, the early Christian era, medieval, and modern philosophy. This pursuit of psychological problems by philosophy constitutes the history of *prescientific psychology*. It can be divided into the following phases:

1. Early Greek thinkers (seventh to fifth century B.C.)
2. Democritus (ca. 460-370 B.C.)
3. Plato's psychology (fourth century B.C.)
4. Aristotelian psychology (fourth century B.C.)
5. Hellenistic period (third to first century B.C.)

6. Final period of pagan philosophy (first to third century)
7. Early Christian thought (up to fifth century)
8. Medieval psychology (from the ninth to fifteenth century)
9. Cartesianism (sixteenth century)
10. Psychology of the seventeeth century
11. Psychology of the eighteenth century
12. Psychology of the nineteenth century

A Quick Glance at the History of Philosophy

Since psychological thought was developed in philosophy, its evolution was part of the evolution of philosophical doctrines. The evolution of philosophy can be briefly and cursorily summarized like this: Philosophy begins in ancient Greece in the seventh century B.C. The great syntheses of the ancient thought appeared later and are represented by Democritus (ca. 460-370 B.C.), Plato (427-347 B.C.), Aristotle (384-322 B.C.), and their systems. Democritus represents Materialism, Plato Idealism, and Aristotle Realism. All three systems were three great fonts of philosophical thought for centuries to come. In the Middle Ages, Thomas Aquinas is the climax of Christian philosophy, developing the Aristotelian philosophy through Christian theology. Then there is a critical turn in the history of philosophy when Descartes (1596-1650) seemingly disregards the philosophical past, builds a new system, and opens the modern era of philosophy. Reaction to Cartesianism is empirical philosophy and the orientations resulting from its inspiration. Then comes the philosophical revolution of Kant and after him the two powerful systems of the nineteenth century, Positivism and Idealism. Keeping this outline in mind, we can proceed now to a few details. We shall presently look into the psychological material contained in the philosophical systems of antiquity and the Middle Ages.

Early Greek Psychology.

The early Greek thinkers, in the seventh, sixth, and fifth centuries B.C., were mainly interested in cosmology, that is, in the nonliving matter and the world around them. Psychological problems were only secondary to these thinkers and referred chiefly to sensation and perception. The latter were treated as natural phenomena and were solved according to the general principles of a given system. We do not find in this early period distinction between matter and spirit. Gradually this distinction appears and is subsequently developed further. It is Anaxagoras (ca. 500-428 B.C.) who is regarded as the first Greek philosopher to suggest a differentiation between the two elements in man, animal, and plant: the spiritual one and the material one. The disparity of the two fundamental elements was crystallized later, in the philosophy of Socrates (469-399 B.C.) and Plato (427-347 B.C.) who were very much preoccupied with man's sensory and intellectual knowledge. In order to explain this knowledge, they focused their attention on the human soul and its spiritual attributes. It is then that the notion of the psyche, the soul, emerges and gradually assumes the meaning which will be subsequently followed and eventually will be made the central object of psychological inquiry.

Democritus

The soul had its place already in the first great synthesis of Greek philosophy, in the synthesis made by Democritus (ca. 460-370 B.C.). He is known as the author of the atomistic doctrine which proclaims that the whole universe, the body and the soul included, is made of the same matter and is composed of small indivisible particles, the atoms. The doctrine is materialistic, and Democritus is called the father of Materialism, because everything that exists and all the phenomena of nature were thought to be of material substance. The soul was also material, and the difference between it and the body lay in the difference in the form of atoms, the atoms of the soul being finer, smoother, and rounder than that of the body. Mental operations were also explained in terms of the atoms and their motion.

Treatises "On the Soul."

Democritus wrote a treatise *On the Soul* which comprised three parts: about the body, about the mind, and about the sentiments. Treatises with this title, *On the Soul*—in Greek *Peri psyches,* in Latin *De anima*—were frequent in antiquity and persisted until the late Middle Ages. They were the early textbooks of psychology. According to the ancient historian of philosophy, Diogenes Laertius, a *Treatise on the Soul* was written by a disciple of Socrates, Simmias of Thebes, but its text has been lost. On the basis of what we know about Simmias, we may surmise that this work might well have been the first systematic dualistic psychology. The most famous is the *Treatise on the Soul* by Aristotle of which an excerpt is presented on page 43. This is the first true psychology in the history of thought. The first Christian treatise of this title was written by Tertullian in about 212. It has been regarded as the "first Christian psychology" but the chief purpose of the author was to refute heretical doctrines about the soul rather than to write a scientific treatise. If there are psychological descriptions of general and philosophical character, they are rather incidental. A passage from this work is presented here. It illustrates the importance of theological considerations based on Revelation so characteristic of all Christian philosophical treatises of this era.

Tertullian, *De anima,* chap. 4
Translated by Edwin A. Quain, S.J.
in *The Fathers of the Church,* Vol. 10

Now that we have decided on the origin of the soul, the next question is as to its nature. When we say that it has its own origin in the breath of God, we obviously hold that the soul had a beginning. Plato denies this, since he believes it to be unborn and uncreated. Since it had beginning, we teach that it was born and made. In this we make no mistake, either, for there is a distinction between being born and being made, and the former term we generally apply to living things. Though such distinctions sometimes indicate that things are mutually exclusive, they may also hint at a certain similarity of meaning. Thus, when we say that something is 'made' we mean that it is 'brought forth,' for anything that receives being in any sense can be said to be generated. Obviously, the maker of anything can be referred to as its parent, and even Plato uses this terminology. So, our faith tells us that souls are made or born. Besides, Plato's opinion is contradicted by Revelation.

Plato

Although much concerned with the soul and its nature, Plato did not write any special treatise on the soul, but his psychological doctrine is scattered through his famous dialogues. We have thirty-five of them of which the most psychological are the *Phaedo,* in which the immortality of the soul is the main theme, the *Phaedrus,* and the *Theaetetus.*

The whole philosophy of Plato began with the analysis of man's knowledge which led to the distinction of two levels, the sensory and the intellectual. From this distinction Plato derived the distinction between the spiritual world and the material world, and together with this, the concept of the human soul. Plato's conclusion was that only the world of ideas is real, the world of matter being merely its shadow or copy. The object of human knowledge is the invisible world of ideas but, as long as man has a body and relies solely on senses, he cannot entirely reach the world of ideas. He learns about it only through its material copy, the visible world. The world of ideas was known to the human soul when the soul lived in it, prior to its earthly existence in a body. The union with a body erased the knowledge of the ideal world, and now the knowledge during the earthly existence of the soul is merely reminiscence of the knowledge acquired in the ideal world, with sensory perception being only an occasion or stimulus to this reminiscence. Learning, then, is actually recollection of what had been previously known but was forgotten. The only valid and proper knowledge comes, therefore, not from senses but from reason. Not attaching much value to the senses as a source of knowledge, and thus to experience and experiment, Plato represented the view which was later combatted and rejected by empirical philosophy.

The soul is imprisoned by the body which hampers and handicaps it. Death separates the two and liberates the soul which returns to the ideal world and lives there eternally. The soul is a complete substance, of divine origin, spiritual, immortal, and eternal. It can live independently of the body to which it is united only accidentally and temporarily. Man in the Platonic doctrine is the soul governing the body. The soul is not of uniform and homogeneous structure though, as it contains three different parts, or functional groups, or levels (from the lowest to the highest), in each of which there are two aspects, the cognitive and the appetitive. Platonic psychology being the product of such a philosophy could not be anything else but spiritualistic and dualistic. In such a psychology, naturally, bodily processes and sensory perceptions were minimized and underestimated.

Platonism created a tradition which continued for many centuries, through Christianity until the arrival of Thomistic philosophy which returned to the realism of Aristotle, to be embodied again in the philosophy of Descartes. Neoplatonism, a system of the third to the beginning of the sixth century, was the direct continuation of Plato's philosophy. In fact all philosophy from the first century B.C. until the thirteenth century, with the exception of only logical studies, was Neoplatonic. Christian theology used this philosophy as the one best suited for the explanation of theological concepts. None of the philosophical systems ever matched the Platonic influence and none made equal contribution to the foundation of the Western culture. Of course not all aspects of Plato's philosophy were equally effective. In general, the spiritualistic and religious elements proved the strongest and lasted longest.

Aristotle and his Psychology.

The genius of Aristotle (384-322 B.C.) has been generally recognized, and he is often called the greatest philosopher of all times. The greatness of Aristotle lies principally in his synthesis and systematization of all the knowledge of his time and in his emphasis on empirical findings. He utilized the investigations of others as well as his own. He was a philosopher and a scientist. His scientific approach and even an experimental bent are revealed in the vast observations, classifications, and definitions of physical and biological phenomena which we find in such works as the *Organon, Physics,* and *History of Animals.* The impact of his philosophy has been felt for over two thousand years, up to the present time.

If anybody can be given the title of the founder of psychology, it is he who would deserve it most because he presented us with the first complete discussion of the mind. Aristotle's system of psychology and influence on psychology were acknowledged by such psychologists as Külpe, Ebbinghaus, and C. S. Meyers, to mention just a few. Külpe stated that "the first truly completed systematic psychology comes from Aristotle." Ebbinghaus said of Aristotle that his amazing genius constructed a psychology which surpassed all other sciences of his epoch. Meyers expresses the opinion that the experimental psychology of the late nineteenth century cannot be called new because "experiment in psychology is at least as old as Aristotle."

The works of Aristotle which hold interest for psychologists are his *De anima* (The Treatise on the Soul), said to be his best work, and a body of smaller treatises called collectively *Parva naturalia*. In *De anima* Aristotle becomes the first historian of psychology when he presents the views of others who were interested in the soul before him, but he also expounds his own views on the nature and activities of the soul. In the *Parva naturalia* he describes and interprets human experience, and even behavior, in concrete terms, on the basis of observation. In these works, especially in *Parva naturalia,* Aristotle is a physiological psychologist rather than a metaphysician as he devotes his attention mainly to biological aspects and to physiological processes of man. This attitude is revealed in the titles of the treatises which comprise the *Parva naturalia*: "On sensation and that which is sensed," "On memory and forgetting," "Concerning sleep and awakening," "Concerning dreams," "Interpretation of dreams," "About a long life and a short life," "Concerning youth and old age," "Concerning life and death," and "About respiration." We shall return to Aristotle when we deal with his hylomorphic doctrine, a basic concept in his psychology.

After Aristotle

After the Aristotelian psychology there was no other original system of psychology in the ancient world. There was, to be sure, much psychological material in the writings of Greek and Roman philosophers but there is no exposition to match the system of Aristotle. There was, for example, a work *On Sense Perception and the Sensory Objects* by Theophrastus in the third century B.C., but we now have only fragments of this work which primarily present the views of the earlier writers. The prevailing approach of the writings in the post-Aristotelian period was eclectic.

There existed, however, a kind of practical psychology represented mainly by the schools of the Stoics and Epicureans. Philosophers of these schools were concerned with practical life, with the wisdom of living, *savoir-vivre*. The metaphysical question, what life is, was not their main problem, it was how to live to either avoid misery (Stoics), or to assure pleasure and happiness (Epicureans) that interested them. They studied human emotions and passions and prescribed rules and methods of handling them to the best interest of the individual. Their psychology aimed at securing a harmonious happy life for the individual. Occasionally they turned their attention to more basic psychological problems. Lucretius, a Roman poet of the first century B.C., whose aim was to expound Epicurean teachings, gives his views on perception and sources of human knowledge.

The Christian Era

In the first centuries of the Christian era not Aristotelian philosophy, but the philosophy of Plato and Neoplatonism held sway. The focus of attention in the Christian thought was on the religious and moral aspects of man and his life. The Christian authors of the first seven centuries, called Fathers of the Church, and the theologians and philosophers of this, as well as of the later period, when they treated of man, were concerned principally with the spiritual nature of the soul, man's relation to God, and his eternal salvation. The psychological processes as such were of secondary interest. In their writings, however, we frequently come across profound analyses of man's inner experiences, spiritual development, and affective life. We find a good example of this kind of analysis in the writings of *St. Augustine* (354-430), bishop of Hippo, especially in his spiritual autobiography, the famous *Confessions*. This autobiography gained for him the title of the first modern psychologist. The reasons for this title were Augustine's penetrating self-analysis, his deep delving into his own emotions, thoughts, memories, and motives, reported with sincerity and in a manner which modern man easily understands and finds familiar despite a lapse of fifteen centuries.

Scholastic Philosophy

The lack of systematic treatment of psychology continues until the Middle Ages. A radical change in Christian thought, both in theology and philosophy, occurred in the Middle Ages when Scholastic philosophy was born. The majority of the philosophers of that period abandoned the Platonic orientation and boldly turned instead to the Aristotelian philosophy, adopting it as their basis. The hylomorphic doctrine of Aristotle was studied again, and became further developed, particularly by *Thomas Aquinas* (1225-1274). This philosopher examined all the philosophical thought of the past, as well as of his time, and built a new system which incorporated elements from the Greek, Jewish, and Arabic philosophy. The philosophical principles of Aristotle were the inspiration of his system. The psychology of Thomas Aquinas is contained mainly in his *Commentary on Aristotle's De Anima,* and in the first part of his monumental work *Summa Theologiae,* which part is often referred to as *The Treatise on Man.* For Aquinas, psychology is a study of human nature, through the analysis of man's acts, powers, and habits. The basic characteristic of man's nature is the integration of the vegetative,

25

sensitive, and spiritual elements of man. Observation and real life experiences were used by Aquinas in his study of man's nature and functions. While the focal point of Aristotle's psychological inquiry is the soul, the emphasis of Thomistic psychology is the nature of man, who in its interpretation is the besouled body. Allied to this notion is the main characteristic of Aquinas' psychology: insistence on the unity of man despite the presence in him of two elements, the bodily and the spiritual. This unity he discusses and explains in the spirit of Aristotelian hylomorphism.

Psychologies of the medieval period followed the trend initiated by Thomas Aquinas. They are rather metaphysical with only scanty references to biological or physiological aspects of human nature. The problems are solved by reasoning rather than by observation, experience, introspection, or induction. An example of the Scholastic psychology of the end of the Middle Ages is a large *Treatise on the Soul* by F. Suarez (1548-1617).

Juan Luis Vives

During the Renaissance great prominence was achieved by Juan Luis Vives (1492-1540), a humanist, a friend of Thomas More and Erasmus, and an unusually talented man who proposed social and educational reforms, which impress us today for their progressiveness. In every book he wrote, he stressed the importance of the understanding of the human mind for education, philosophy, politics, and science, and he proved himself a master of introspection and observation. He was considered by many as the greatest psychologist of his time and of the next three centuries. Vives was described as "the father of modern psychology" and the forerunner of the dynamic psychology of the twentieth century.

His claim to fame in psychology is his most significant book,

26

De anima et vita ("About the Mind and Life," 1538). It has three parts—the first devoted to association of ideas, learning, memory; the second, to the rational soul and its faculties; and the third, to feelings and emotions. The book contains a wealth of keen observation about human nature in general. The most original part of the book is that which pertains to the association of ideas. A Scottish philosopher of the nineteenth century, Sir William Hamilton, recognized this when he said that "Vives' observations comprise in brief, nearly all of principal moment that has been said upon this subject (of mental association) either before or since."

The Dawn of Modern Psychology

The seventeenth century brings a definite change in the treatment of psychological problems. Observation and induction now supplant metaphysical analysis and deduction. Psychology decidedly ceases to be the science of the soul, and instead, the mind and its operations come to the fore. This change is associated with Descartes. Along with the new trend psychology assumes a more important role within philosophy, and more attention is given to strictly psychological problems. This trend grew so much stronger that philosophy, it was said, became psychological, particularly from the eighteenth century on. Before we enter into this phase in the next chapters we must acquaint ourselves with the man who epitomizes the new tradition in philosophy and science, Descartes.

Descartes.

René Descartes (Latin name: Cartesius) (1596-1650) was both a philosopher and a scientist. Although his achievements in mathematics and the natural sciences were not small, he is principally known for his role in the history of philosophy. Revolting against traditional philosophy and rejecting all philosophical systems which preceded him, he developed a new system independent of any previous system, thereby opening a new era in philosophy, which came to be called the era of modern philosophy. Philosophy at his time had become sterile, consisting of mere repetition of the views of old masters, and confined to pure speculations. It was incapable of keeping pace with the rapidly developing scientific study of nature. The rebellion of Descartes against traditional philosophy was expressed by his total rejection of the whole philosophical past, particularly Scholasticism as he knew it, and by his decision to build philosophy anew, "to cast aside the loose earth and sand that I may reach the rock or clay," as he said of himself. He looked for a solid foundation on which he could build his system. The only unquestionable fact for him at the beginning of his philosophical inquiry was his own doubt about everything. This doubt naturally implied that he was thinking, and if he was thinking—he argued—then he must have real existence for there could be no thinking without someone who actually thinks. This discovery of Descartes is expressed in his celebrated statement, the starting point of his philosophy, "Cogito, ergo sum." "I think, hence I exist." Here is his own description of his mental discourse which led him to this conclusion:

While we thus reject all of which we can entertain the smallest doubt, and even imagine that it is false, we easily, indeed, suppose that there is neither God, nor sky, nor bodies, and that we ourselves have neither hands nor feet, nor, finally, a body, but we cannot in the same way suppose that we *are not,* while we doubt of the truth of those things; for there is a repugnance in conceiving that what thinks does not exist at the very time when it thinks. Accordingly, the knowledge, 'I think, therefore, I exist', is the first and most important certain principle that occurs to me. (*Discours de la méthode*)

The Psychology of Descartes

In the writings of Descartes there is a great deal of psychological material, especially in his *Passions de l'âme* ("Passions of the Soul," 1629) and *Traité de l'homme* ("Treatise of Human Nature," 1662). For him man was a soul and a body. The soul was spiritual and the body was material and acted like a machine. He was concerned with, and discussed sensation, emotions, operations of the mind, ideas and their origin. His knowledge of anatomy and physics allowed him to understand better the functions of the sense organs, particulary of the eye. The subject of psychology, according to Descartes, is not man but the spiritual mind of man and its contents. The mind has three functions: intellectual cognition, volition, and sensation. The only method of studying the mind is an analysis of consciousness. Mind does not comprise anything but conscious states. Very characteristic of the Cartesian system and essential to its comprehension is its doctrine of innate ideas.

Innate Ideas

There are mainly two reasons for the explanation of innate ideas here. First, since innate ideas were the principal object of attack by empirical philosophy, we come, through the discussion of them to a better appreciation of the difference between Cartesianism and empiricism. Empirical philosophy exerted most of its efforts to prove the opposite to innate ideas, namely, that the human mind is completely blank at birth and that all the acquired knowledge in one's lifetime comes through senses. Secondly, we are interested in innate ideas because this concept survived in psychology in the form of an orientation which is referred to as nativism.

Knowledge is possible, according to Descartes, because man is richly endowed from his birth with innate ideas which constitute an indispensable basis and prerequisite for the acquisition of knowledge. These ideas are not necessarily actual knowledge of things, but rather intuitive knowledge of principles, or inclinations and potentialities which the soul possesses for knowing things. The idea of infinity is such an innate idea. So is, "I think, hence I exist." Innate ideas exist in every mind regardless of experience. They are to be recognized, uncovered, and utilized in man's thinking. Where do they come from? They are implanted in the mind, or more exactly in the soul since Descartes equated mind with the soul, by God the Creator of the soul. Sensory experience is only secondary in the acquisition of knowledge because it is only an occasion, a stimulus, for awakening the innate idea. Descartes kept modifying his views on this matter in his writings, but the fundamental concept of innate ideas remained an integral part of his philosophy.

Nativism

Nativism in psychology was an echo of the Cartesian innate ideas. Psychologists and all those who referred to mental processes sometimes invoked innate ideas to account for certain processes and phenomena of mind. Johannes Müller, the physiologist of the nineteenth century, thought that space perception was an inherited habit and that experience was not the essential factor in the perception of space. Helmholtz, who studied vision and hearing, thought the opposite and considered experience as the source of space perception. His view represented what has been called empiricism in contrast to nativism. The empiricism-nativism antinomy has been reflected in various problems of psychology, and has tended to divide psychologists into nativists and empiricists. In the history of psychology, Carl Stumpf and the Gestalt school can be cited as followers of the nativistic doctrine. In America

William James was also a nativist. The debates and the investigations purporting to support one view or the other by experimental evidence, are far from ended. In the field of perception the issue is still much discussed and is usually expressed now as the problem of past experience or learning versus innate organizing processes.

The Impact of Cartesianism

The imprint that Cartesianism left on subsequent generations was extensive and profound. Many trends and doctrines which appeared after Descartes can be traced directly to him. Rationalism, intellectualism, subjectivism, nativism, introspectionism, all were more or less fathered by the Cartesian philosophy or more specifically by Cartesian dualism. The dual aspect of his system, the spiritualistic and the materalistic, was the source of two streams of philosophical thought, the idealistic and the mechanistic.

The effect of this philosophy can be felt even today. The numerous publications which appeared all over the world in connection with the 300th anniversary of Descartes' death (in 1950) testified that Descartes is still alive today in his influence on modern thought. At least the issues he raised are discussed today and his views are still seriously debated not only by philosophers, but likewise by modern psychologists and physiologists. Although there are no strict Cartesians, the approaches to the solution of many problems remain Cartesian. Of all domains, psychology probably has felt the impact of the philosophy of Descartes most.

As viewed by twentieth century philosophy, the effect of Cartesian philosophy and of the seventeenth century philosophy in general was on the whole harmful. A. N. Whitehead (1861-1947), the great mathematician and philosopher of our century, in his *Science and the Modern World* (1925), speaks

31

of the philosophy of the seventeenth century as the font and origin of many errors whose "quite unbelievable" set of "scientific abstractions" has ruined modern philosophy.

The Effect of Cartesian Dualism on Psychology.

The aspect of Cartesian psychology which is of special interest to us is its dualism. We shall come to this point in the next chapter. Cartesian dualism together with the treament of the body-mind problem by Descartes and its effect on the psychology of the next generations are a vital chapter in the history of psychology. Cartesian dualism became prevalent and strongly embedded in psychological thought. All who subscribed to dualism in principle, and among them the builders of the new psychology, followed the Cartesian form of dualism. It was this Cartesian dualism which dominated the early psychology and which can still be detected in some psychological theories of today.

The New Era of Psychology.

This chapter traced the philosophical roots from the ancient era to the beginning of the modern era. We endeavored to point out along our route some salient developments of pre-scientific psychology. We can refer to them as the *remote* roots of psychology. Now we shall discuss the *immediate* roots of scientific psychology. Our approach is as follows: First we shall ascertain the fundamental characteristics of psychology at the time when it separated from philosophy. Secondly, we shall show how these characteristics originated from philosophy. In this way we hope to make the whole character of the early scientific psychology more understandable. It should be borne in mind that when in the future the psychologists who were dissatisfied with the above characteristics and tried to modify its character or completely abandon this particular kind of psychology, they at the same time disavowed and attacked the underlying philosophical doctrine.

The Characteristics of the New Psychology.

When the young psychology of the nineteenth century emerged from philosophy, it had the following basic characteristics:

1. It was *dualistic,* that is, it viewed man as a composite of body and mind.
2. It was *empirical* and *experimental,* that is, it made experience and experiment its basic sources of knowledge and methods of scientific inquiry.
3. It was *sensationistic,* which meant that it relied heavily on sensation, and major interests and objects of study were sensation and perception.
4. It was *associationistic* because it regarded association as the fundamental process of mind and it proceeded to explain all mental life and even mind itself on this basis.

These characteristics describe psychology well at the time of its emancipation from philosophy and for many years thereafter. Their philosophical parentage is undeniable. The second and the third characteristics are also associated with the influence of physiology but this influence would have been neither possible nor effective if the philosophical preparation had not been already present. These four above-mentioned characteristics, in other words, make sense only in the light of philosophical ancestry. It is for this reason that we shall discuss, in the same sequence, systems and issues of philosophy whence these characteristics grew, namely:

1. *Dualism* and the body-mind problem with its various solutions offered by philosophers.

2. *Empiricism* or empirical philosophy.
3. *Sensationism* or the emphasis on *the study of sensation and perception in philosophy.*
4. *Associationism.*

The above philosophical doctrines were the ones which made the most profound impact on psychology. In the succeeding chapters we shall discuss them not in chronological order, but in the sequence given above. In addition to these major fonts of philosophical influence, there were other philosophical systems which affected psychological thought. Among them were the philosophical systems of the nineteenth century, some antedating the birth of psychology and others contemporary with the already growing psychology. In reviewing the philosophies, we shall not be concerned with their significance in the history of philosophy or with their critique and evaluation, but only with the manner in which they influenced psychology. Our task here is not to evaluate philosophical theories but to show their effect on psychological thought and, in this way, to shed some light on the understanding of the origins of scientific psychology.

While discussing the immediate philosophical roots of psychology, we make no special attempt to distinguish specific philosophical influences peculiar to the psychology of individual countries. It is well to note that each country, besides sharing the general streams of thought with other countries, had its own unique currents or emphases which might have been particularly powerful in molding the psychology of this country. Sometimes it is desirable to study and refer to, not the philosophical systems or ideas of a particular time, but to the social background and cultural atmosphere in which they operated, as often only the latter can give us the key to the understanding of their influence. When we consider one country after another we find that not only each of them added its own color to the principal philosophical ideas but the degree of effectiveness of these ideas on the mind of the country varied a great deal. Hence it may be said that the psychology of each country had its own philosophical antecedents and confirmation of this fact is easily found when these antecedents of such countries as Germany, Britain, France, and the United States are scrutinized. It is obvious that we cannot do justice to all these antecedents but we shall indicate them occasionally. Our main effort, however, will be directed toward tracing only the major philosophical doctrines and their general effect on the science of psychology.

SUMMARY

The highlights of the prescientific psychology were presented in historical order. Early Greek psychology consisted of a description of sensory cognition. The distinction between soul and mind gradually emerges and the soul is defined. A materialistic definition was formulated by Democritus, the idealistic by Plato, and the realistic, or hylomorphistic, by Aristotle. The latter is the author of the first system of psychology. In the Christian era, the soul is mainly a subject of theology and ethics. Otherwise, there is an absence of an original psychological system until the Scholastics. In Scholastic philosophy the emphasis is on metaphysics: the soul is a metaphysical entity. The philosophy of Descartes marks the shift from the metaphysics of soul to the study of mind. The impact of Cartesianism on subsequent psychology was profound. Early scientific Psychology bears marks of philosophical influence in its characteristics, namely, in being dualistic, empirical and experimental, sensationistic, and associationistic.

35

SYNOPSIS OF THE PSYCHOLOGICAL THOUGHT IN PHILOSOPHY

from ancient Greece to Descartes.

Philosophical Doctrines	Characteristics	Time
1. Early Greek	Main interest is cosmology. Speculation about sensation.	7th to 5th century B.C.
2. Anaxagoras	Early distinction between the soul and the body.	ca. 500-428 B.C.
3. Democritus	Materialistic and atomistic interpretation of the soul, its nature and operation.	ca. 460-370 B.C.
4. Plato	Spritualistic and dualistic psychology. Gulf between the soul and the body.	427-347 B.C.
5. Aristotle	The first system of psychology. The soul is the vital principle of the body. Both substantially united.	384-322 B.C.
6. Christian philosophy	The soul is considered from religious and moral viewpoints.	1st to 9th century
7. Scholasticism	The soul is studied in its nature and relation to the body. Aristotelian psychology is revived by Thomas Aquinas.	9th to 15th century
8. Vives	Forerunner of modern psychology.	1492-1540
9. Descartes	The revival of Platonic psychology. Radical dualism. Nativism.	1596-1650

36

3

Dualism and the Body-Mind Problem

After having reviewed the continuity of psychological thought in pre-modern philosophy from the chronological point of view, we shall now take a different viewpoint. We shall consider those issues and doctrines of modern philosophy which were directly related to the psychology of the nineteenth century and preceded its origin as a separate science. They were: the dualistic doctrine and the body-mind problem; empiricism; sensationism; and associationism. They constitute the immediate roots of psychology. The psychology of the nineteenth century was their direct product. Therefore, they are the ones which best explain the character and orientation of the new psychology at the time when it arose. In this chapter we shall discuss one of the most important of these issues and doctrines, the body-mind problem, for it had the greatest impact of longest duration on psychological thought. This body-mind problem has also been one of the most baffling and exasperating problems of philosophy.

The chapter is divided into two parts. The first part will explain the meaning of the body-mind problem and present a brief history of dualistic doctrines. The second part will analyse the effect and consequences of dualism in psychology.

A. THE MEANING AND HISTORY OF DUALISM

The Meaning of Dualism

The new psychology of the nineteenth century was in general dualistic, for it viewed man as a composite of body and mind and consistently distinguished in him, if not the soul and the body, at least between the bodily and the mental. The term dualism (*duo,* two) has been defined in various ways. To avoid any misunderstanding as to its meaning in the context of our discussion and for the convenience of this discussion we define dualism here as any doctrine which assumes that man is composed of two distinct and different elements. It is contrasted with monism (*monos,* one) which denies such a distinction and proclaims complete homogeneity of human nature.

It will be remembered that the first philosopher to suggest a distinction of elements in man, as well as in animals and plants, was *Anaxagoras* (about 500-428 B.C.) when he referred to their composition of *nous,* or mind, and of material organism. The first philosopher to make the distinction clear and to discuss it systematically was *Plato* (427-347 B.C.). He is therefore called the originator of dualism, which thereafter persisted in one form or another and served as one of the basic tenets of almost all philosophical systems up to the seventeenth century. Since philosophical dualism usually recognized the existence of the spiritual element in man, the soul, it was consequently favored and supported by religion and theological systems.

An opposite doctrine, suggested quite early in ancient philosophy and eventually fully formulated in the modern era, namely monism, held that man is one complete indivisible entity, and there are no distinguishable, separable elements in him. Depending on their fundamental viewpoint, spiritualistic or materialistic, the adherents of monism may be divided into two classes: some regarded man as a purely material entity, not different essentially from other creatures and from the rest of the universe, whereas the others viewed man as an entirely spiritual substance. The former view has been called materialistic monism, the latter spiritualistic monism. Monism gained favor in the eighteenth century, and materialistic monism, spurred by the progress of the natural sciences and evolutionism, became particularly strong in the nineteenth and twentieth centuries. We shall return to monism again later.

Body-Mind Problem.

Dualism created the so-called body-mind problem, or the problem of the relationship of the two distinct components of human nature, the soul or mind, and the body. Once such a dualistic assumption was made, the explanation of the mutual relationship of the mind and the body became necessary. It was natural to ask how two such different elements could co-exist, one of which was immaterial, unextended, and independent of matter, and the other material, extended, and subject to all physical forces. Do they influence each other, and if they do, how is such influence possible when these elements are so different, and how is it realized? These and similar questions about the relationship of the two elements in man constitute the body-mind problem. The most acute form of this problem resulted from the Cartesian dualism and hence after Descartes it is given special attention by philosophers.

The body-mind problem has been called the perennial problem of philosophy because it is found in every phase of the history of philosophy and because every philosophical system took a position with regard to it. It has always been a crucial problem whenever man's nature was studied. It was also a serious and urgent problem because an answer to this problem has, as William McDougall said in his *Body and Mind,* "some bearing upon fundamental doctrines of religion and upon our estimate of man's position and destiny in the world."

Various answers and solutions of the body-mind problem have been offered in the course of the history of philosophy. We are going to present those solutions which from the historical standpoint were the most important for psychology: Aristotle's Hylomorphism, Descartes' Interactionism, and the Psychophysical Parallelism. While discussing these doctrines we shall also speak of their proponents which will give us the opportunity to mention their other contributions to psychology.

Aristotle's Hylomorphism

The starting point of Plato's philosophy of man was the difference between the spiritual and the material elements in man. This differentiation in man was the outcome of his analysis of man's two levels of knowledge, the sensory and the intellectual. He then proceeded to explain how the two elements were able to coexist in man and constitute one person. His disciple, Aristotle (384-322 B.C.), on the other hand, took as his starting point the unity of man and only upon analysis of man's nature did he discover its complexity and recognize in him the existence of two principles. His philosophy of man, to be properly comprehended, has to be viewed in the light of his most fundamental concept, the metaphysical dichotomy of potency and act, and with the notion of matter and form which exemplified this dichotomy.

All material things, according to Aristotle, is composed of matter and form. Neither can exist by itself, each complements the other. Matter must have form, and form must be related to matter. Both are interdependent and when united, form one substance. Form determines the kind of substance and its characteristics. To illustrate this point Aristotle gave an example of a piece of bronze. The bronze must have some shape in order to exist. This shape may be a sphere, or a statue

40

of Apollo, or a misshapen mass. Without some kind of shape, the bronze cannot possibly exist. On the other hand, the shape has no existence of its own. This formulation is known as the hylomorphic (*hyle*, matter; *morphe*, form) doctrine of Aristotle. It is the cornerstone of all Aristotelian philosophy and psychology.

Aristotle taught that all living beings, plants, animals, and man, have a soul which is their form. Being the form, the soul is the source of all vital activities, all the characteristics, also the reason for the unity and integration of all functions for the benefit of the whole organism and its ends. The human soul is the highest form of soul because it is endowed with ability to think. The union of the body and the soul is a substantial union of matter and form. Being so united the soul and the body form a single, complete, and integrated substance which exists and acts as a unit. It is a far cry from the Platonic doctrine which considered the soul and the body distinct and separable substances, and man as the soul "imprisoned by the body." Since according to Aristotelian doctrine, man is one substance, each of his processes or actions, be it thinking, perceiving, walking, or digesting, is the activity of the whole man, that is, of the body as well as of the soul.

Thomas Aquinas further developed the hylomorphic doctrine in conjunction with his metaphysical principles and used them in explaining the spiritual character of human nature. He thus went further than Aristotle when he explicitly affirmed the spirituality and immortality of the human soul. Christian philosophers who accepted the hylomorphic doctrine of Aristotle understood it usually in the Thomistic interpretation.

The Aristotelian doctrine lies between spiritualism and materialism. It is rather a synthesis of both these views than merely a juxtaposition of spiritualistic and materialistic prin-

41

ciples or neutrality with respect to them. It is not an artificial combination of two theories, resulting from an intense desire of effecting a compromise in a dilemma. It is a genuine and original synthesis in logical harmony with all Aristotelian philosophy. One gets the impression that when some writers of the nineteenth century analysed the body-mind problem and referred to Aristotle, they did not quite grasp the full meaning of the hylomorphic doctrine as applied to man. This was perhaps because they knew it through biased philosophers who in their writings did not do justice to Aristotelian Psychophysics.

Three characteristic references of Aristotle to the nature of the soul:

Because all knowledge is in our estimation a thing of beauty and worth, and because this is more particularly true of those types of knowledge which are more exact in themselves or which refer to more excellent or more remarkable objects; on both these grounds we are justified in ranking psychology, or a study of the soul, among the first of our interests. Moreover, it is commonly agreed that a knowledge of this subject contributes greatly to the general discovery of truth, especially in the domain of nature; for the soul is, as it were, the 'moving principle' of animal life. Our aim is to discover and understand, first the nature and essence of the soul, and next its various properties, some of which are held to be attributes peculiar to the soul itself, others to belong to the 'whole animal' by virtue of the soul's presence in it.

* * *

There is a certain type of entity to which we give the name 'thing,' and by this word we may mean either: (1) matter, which in itself has not the character of a 'this,' or (2) the shape and essential form by which we distinguish this thing from that, or (3) the whole, which comprises of the latter there are in turn two kinds, illustrated by the possession of knowledge as distinguished from its active exercise.

The most generally recognized class of substances is that of bodies—

42

especially natural bodies, which are the originals of all others. Some natural bodies possess life, others do not; life signifying the power of self-nourishment, and of growth and decay. Accordingly, every natural body possessing life must be not only a 'specific thing' but one comprising both matter and form. But because body thus possesses a certain attribute, namely life, it is not on that account to be identified with the soul; for body is not itself an attribute but simply the subject and the material basis of attributes. Soul, therefore, must be a specific thing in the sense that it is the form of a natural body endowed with the capacity of life. Specific "thinghood" in this sense is actuality; and soul, therefore, is the actuality of body as just defined. . . .

* * *

The soul may be defined as *the initial actuality of a natural body endowed with the capacity of life.*

Reprinted from *Aristotle,* translated and edited by Philip Wheelwright, by permission of The Odyssey Press, Inc., New York.

The Cartesian Dualism

The Aristotelian psychophysics was to be overshadowed from the seventeenth century on by the Cartesian philosophy of man. We spoke of Descartes in the previous chapter. We realize already that the place which Descartes occupies in the history of human thought is unique. His philosophy constituted an end of one phase of this history and a beginning of a new one. It tried to demolish the whole philosophical past and erect a structure which was to be the philosophic framework for future philosophy. Of all Descartes' views, his dualistic doctrine was the one which had the most far-reaching consequences for psychology.

It is not the whole philosophical system of Descartes but his philosophy of human nature which claims our attention here. It may be summarized in the following way: Man is a composite of a material body and a spiritual soul. The body is like a machine or automaton governed by the laws of mechanics. Its functions and movements are executed by material energies or forces called *animal spirits*. Produced in the brain, moved by the heat of the heart, these animal spirits travel along the nerves which are hollow tubes, and reach the muscles and put them into action. The soul is spiritual and independent of its material body. It is the ultimate source of life in man. Its influence reaches the body through the pineal gland which Descartes thought was "the seat of the soul."

Such a view made man a creature composed of two separate entities, each of completely different nature. Man was not one substance but two complete substances living side by side yet having nothing in common. Such a system denied the unity and singleness of human nature. This extreme dualism, that is, this antithesis between the soul and the body, despite the difficulties it entailed with respect to the mutual dealings of the soul and the body, was nevertheless generally accepted, and dominated modern philosophy up to the end of the nineteenth century for reasons to be discussed later.

Descartes, *Meditations*
Excerpts from the Med. VI. Translated by J. Veitch

... If the body of man be considered as a kind of machine, so made up and composed of bones, nerves, muscles, veins, blood, and skin, that although there were in it no mind, it would still exhibit the same motions which it at present manifests involuntarily, and therefore without the aid of the mind, (and simply by the dispositions of its organs) ...

... There is a vast difference between mind and body, in respect that body, from its nature, is always divisible, and that mind is entirely indivisible ...

... The mind does not immediately receive the impression from all the parts of the body, but only from the brain, or perhaps even from one small part of it, viz., that in which the common sense is said to be ...

44

... Nature teaches me by these sensations of pain, hunger, thirst, etc., that I am not only lodged in my body as a pilot in a vessel, but that I am besides so intimately conjoined, and as it were intermixed with it, that my mind and body compose a certain unity. For if this were not the case, I should not feel pain when my body is hurt...

The Difficulties with the Cartesian Doctrine of Interaction.

Cartesian dualism was part of the philosophical heritage which penetrated early psychological thinking. Philosophers tried to explain how the soul and the body influenced each other in their coexistence in man, and various solutions were offered. Descartes' own explanation gave origin to the *doctrine of interaction,* which spoke of the soul and the body as acting directly on each other. But it was abandoned even by his most ardent disciples as it presented insurmountable difficulties. Aside from the fact that it was always hard to conceive how a spiritual and unextended substance could act upon a material and extended substance, and vice versa, in the nineteenth century the interactionism of Descartes appeared incapable of reconciliation with physics. The influence of the soul on the body through the pineal gland was the influence from outside, from another world, the immaterial world. This implied a constant influx of *material* energy from an immaterial source and such a new influx of energy clashed with the physicists' principle of the conservation of energy in the physical universe.

The admirers and followers of Descartes proposed other solutions. While adhering to the Cartesian dualism they tried to obviate its difficulties and to find a way out of the body-mind dilemma. Among the new systems, the most influential were: the Occasionalism of *Geulincx* (1625-1669), the Ontologism of *Malebranche* (1638-1715), the Pantheism of *Spinoza* (1632-1677), and the theory of Preestablished

Harmony of *Leibnitz* (1646-1716). All these systems proposed their own solutions of the body-mind problem with formulations consistent with their own fundamental principles. As interesting as they may be for a historian of philosophy, they need not concern us here, for their influence on modern psychology with one exception was not apparent. Only one of the proposed solutions should interest us here because it gave roots to an important theory embraced later by all great pioneers of psychology. It was the Leibnitzian theory of *Preestablished Harmony* and *Parallelism*. Leibnitzian parallelism was the beginning of *Psychophysical Parallelism,* formulated by Alexander Bain around 1860, and accepted by early psychologists implicity if not explicitly as their basic philosophical view on the nature of man. We will discuss it later.

Leibnitz

Gottfried Wilhelm Leibnitz (1646-1716) was a philosopher, a mathematician, a politician, and one of the most learned men of his time. In philosophy he was influenced to a great extent by Descartes. As such he accepted the Cartesian distinction between the soul and the body but his solution of the body-mind problem was his own original idea. Known as the theory of parallelism it was the consequence of his more basic doctrine of *Preestablished Harmony.*

Parallelism

The concept of the universe as presented by Leibnitz was a pluralistic one, that is, he believed that the world was composed of innumerable different substances, of the same nature but of different degrees of perfection, *monads,* which are simple, unextended, dynamic, but completely independent of each other and without any effect on each other. Each monad is like a small universe of its own. The human soul is such a monad,

46

and the body is an aggregate of monads which the soul dominates. Both the soul and body act together for the same purpose. How this cooperation is possible Leibnitz explains by the harmonious order established among the monads by God. He created the soul and the body, and established a perfect harmony between them so that their activities parallel one another perfectly. All the activities of the soul have their exact counterpart in the activities of the body. Both activities are in perfect harmony and in accurate parallel but without any causal relationship. Perception corresponds and is parallel to the functioning of the sense organs, and the motions of the body take place as the soul wills. The body and the soul are like two clocks, Leibnitz illustrates, which although completely independent show exactly the same time because they were wound and regulated by the same hand.

The theory of Preestablished Harmony itself did not find wide support. The concept of parallelism between the spiritual and the material universe, however, strongly appealed to philosophers who, clinging to Cartesian dualism, were anxious to find a more satisfactory answer to the body-mind problem than the ones offered thus far. This concept, transformed into Psychophysical Parallelism, gained popularity with psychologists of the nineteenth century.

Leibnitzian Heritage.

Leibnitzian philosophy serves as a good illustration of how philosophical ideas are echoed in psychology. Its parallelism was transformed into the Psychophysical Parallelism of the nineteenth century. Its insistence on activity as the essential characteristic of substances was revived in the *act psychology* initiated by *F. Brentano* in the second half of the nineteenth century, and later characterized such psychologies as that of W. James and W. McDougall. It also foreshadowed the ideas of the unconscious and prepared for the notion of apperception. Leibnitz taught that substances have different degrees of consciousness. There is the initial stage, the "little perceptions," in themselves unconscious, which sum up, become conscious, and reach their final actualization in *apperception*. This conception of the degrees of consciousness—the transition from the unconscious to the conscious—was taken directly from Leibnitz by Johann Friedrich Herbart (1776-1841), professor of philosophy at Göttingen, and it foreshadowed Freud's own concept of the unconscious. Herbart who represents the transformation period of philosophical psychology into physiological psychology in Germany, and who significantly influenced the originator of psychology, Wundt, borrowed and developed other ideas from Leibnitz. One of them, the notion of apperception, was made a very basic one in German psychology. Apperception, a term invented by Leibnitz, was defined by this psychology as a process by which past experiences were combined with new perceptions.

Christian Wolff.

The immediate continuator of Leibnitz was Christian von Wolff (1679-1754) who deserves notice as the first to draw a distinction between empirical and rational psychology which has been held since and to write two separate treatises of these two branches. He also foresaw the possibility of a mathematical branch of psychology and he called this new branch *psychometria*. The possibility of introducing mathematics and measurement into psychology was developed further again by Herbart. H. Lotze, Herbart's successor in the chair of philosophy at Göttingen, and G. E. Müller, Lotze's successor, and Ebbinghaus, and most particularly, Fechner (who said of himself that in the ashes of Herbart's fire he had found some coals for his own hearth) represent the early trend towards a quantitative approach and measurement in psychology. In the light of these facts we see that the effect of Leibnitzian philosophy, mainly through the mediation of Herbart, was considerable.

The First Attempt at Experimental Psychology.

Coming back to Wolff we may observe that the indebtedness of modern psychology to him is perhaps greater than is ordinarily thought because the earliest plea for an experimental psychology, antedating Wundt by over a hundred years, bears a strong mark of influence by and similarity to Wolff's *Empirical Psychology*. We refer to J. G. Krüger's (1715-1759) *Attempt at an Experimental Psychology* published in 1756 which was brought to the attention of the historians of psychology only recently by A. Mintz (1954). In it Krüger calls for experimentation in psychology and the inclusion of facts from medicine. Krüger's book appears to be the first known attempt to establish a psychology based on the experimentation and findings of physiology.

B.   THE FATE OF DUALISM

Let us now summarize the history of dualism and attempt an evaluation of its effect on psychology. In doing so, we hope to make more understandable the final transformation of dualism into psychological parallelism, the principal doctrine of the new psychology, and the whole body-mind issue of modern psychology.

The Phases of Dualism.

Dualism as a concept is as old as human thought, both philosophical and theological. Philosophy until the nineteenth century, as has been emphasized before, was predominantly dualistic, there being two main forms of dualism which ran through the various philosophical systems. One, the extreme form, in-

49

THE BODY-MIND PROBLEM

Name	Theory	Form	View	Representatives
MONISM	Existence of only *one* principle in man: body *or* soul	IDEALISM	*Spiritual soul* is the only reality	Berkeley, idealists of the 19th century; Hegel
		MATERIALISM	*Material body* is the only reality	Hobbes, de La Mettrie, Cabanis, Moleschott, Haeckel
DUALISM	Existence of *two* different principles in man: body *and* soul.	HYLOMORPHISM	Body and soul form *one substance*	Aristotle, Thomas Aquinas, Neoscholastics
		INTERACTIONISM	Body and soul are *two substances interacting*	Descartes
		PARALLELISM	Body and soul are *two substances acting independently*	Leibnitz
		PSYCHOPHYSICAL PARALLELISM	Body and mind are *two different aspects* of man.	Bain, Wundt

50

DIAGRAMMATIC REPRESENTATION OF THE MAIN BODY-MIND THEORIES

INTERACTIONISM:
Body and mind are different and separate but influence each other.

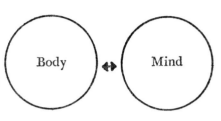

PARALLELISM:
Body and mind are distinct and separate, do not influence each other but bodily and mental activities are perfectly correlated.

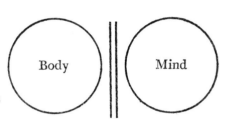

HYLOMORPHISM:
Body and mind make one complete substance.

DOUBLE-ASPECT THEORIES:
Man is an organism which manifests two different aspects: bodily and mental

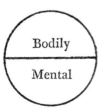

troduced by Plato, postulated the existence of two completely different entities in man, the soul and the body, which remain permanently separated as two distinct substances. It continued in the Neoplatonic philosophy of the first centuries of the Christian era and in all the systems which built on the Platonic philosophy. The other form, the moderate, was the contribution of Aristotle. It distinguished between the two principles, the body and the soul, but saw them united in man, forming one complete substance. Philosophies which followed the Aristotelian doctrine, Scholastic philosophy in particular, preserved this form of dualism.

Descartes reverted to extreme dualism, rejecting the teachings of the great Scholastics, and made this dualism even more explicit and radical. In modern philosophy after Descartes we encounter two opposite reactions to this radical dualism: acceptance, with some modification, or dissatisfaction, criticism, and rejection. Most philosophers, until the nineteenth century, especially the German philosophers, one of whom was Leibnitz, subscribed to Cartesian dualism. As Cartesians they differed mainly in the solution of the body-mind problem, in other words, in the way they explained the relationship between body and mind. Scientific thought, particularly biology and physiology, we must note, was also pervaded by the Cartesian dichotomy of man.

We may now mention some reasons why Cartesian dualism could have such a strong grip upon philosophical and scientific thought for almost three centuries. One was the powerful appeal of Cartesian philosophy and the prestige of Descartes, the philosopher and the scientist. Another reason was the convenient division of labor in the study of man, which the extreme dualism of Descartes suggested without necessitating the choice between materialism or spiritualism. The soul and its nature could be studied separately, by theologians and philosophers, without taking body into account. The body, on the other hand, since it was governed by the laws of physics, could be the domain of scientists without any need of recourse to the soul and spiritual forces and without any restraint of theological or philosophical notions. Cartesian dualism obviated the necessity of taking a stand with respect to materialism or spiritualism. It permitted a convenient neutrality with respect to metaphysical and theological theses.

Monism

Let us now consider the other reaction to Cartesian dualism. There was from the very appearance of Cartesian philosophy, a dissatisfaction and even a rebellion against the radicalism of its dualism, voiced in different circles. Some contemporaries of Descartes and thinkers of succeeding generations found his dualism untenable and therefore, instead of continuing in the Cartesian contra-distinction and contradiction, preferred to choose either one of his entities, following either the spiritualistic or the mechanistic aspect of his system. Thus a twofold divergent stream of monistic thought emerged and persisted through the subsequent centuries in the form of philosophical idealism on the one hand, or in the form of materialism on the other hand. The philosophy of the nineteenth century clearly showed the end results of these two divergent streams, gross materialism and exteme idealism.

Materialistic philosophy viewed the universe, man included, as pure matter, subject only to physical laws. The existence of a spiritual world or spiritual forces was denied by this philosophy. Representatives of such a view were Thomas Hobbes (1588-1679), a contemporary of Descartes; in the next century, Julien de La Mettrie (1709-1751) and Pierre J. G. Cabanis (1757-1808), and in the nineteenth century, Jacob Moleschott (1822-1893) and Ernst H. Haeckel (1834-1919). The culmination of this philosophical stream with regard to man was such statements as "there is no thought without phosphorus," "the thought is a product of the brain as a secretion is a product of a gland," "mind, that is, the brain," "man is what he eats."

The other monistic stream, the idealistic, attributed true existence only to the spirit and either denied the reality of matter completely or proclaimed its dependence on the existence of mind. This idealistic philosophy began in modern times with Berkeley (1685-1753), and attained its peak in the German idealists such as Fichte (1762-1814) and Schelling (1775-1854), and particularly in the absolute idealism of Hegel (1770-1831). The latter asserted that the essential nature of reality is only reason, in other words, the only reality is that which exists in the mind. "The rational is the real, and the real is the rational," were Hegel's words.

Persistence of Cartesian Dualism.

Monism, materialistic or idealistic, could not offset the domination of Cartesianism. Despite the monistic philosophical current and its gains, Cartesian dualism continued to permeate both philosophical and scientific thought up to the second half of the nineteenth century and showed strength in some quarters in the twentieth century. M. H. Pirenne's observation, in his study, *Descartes and the Body-Mind Problem in Physiology,* in 1950, that many physiologists "appear . . . to adhere to the Cartesian doctrine, but few state it openly," may be applied to psychologists of the past and perhaps to some of today. It certainly applies to the founders of the new psychology who explicitly or implicitly adhered to it. In the later part of the nineteenth century a strong attack against the Cartesian domination came from the Neo-Aristotelians and Neoscholastics. Neoscholastic philosophy ended Cartesian influence among the philosophers of the Catholic Church. Further opposition, a revolt, as some historians of philosophy termed it, was launched by several philosophical quarters in the twentieth century. Baffled and frustrated by the troublesome body-mind problem, some of them decided to ignore it or bypass it. Frequently the label "pseudo-problem" was attached to it. Psychology, however, could not escape it easily, and continually, willingly or unwillingly, had to face it.

Psychology and Dualism.

Psychology by virtue of its subject matter was naturally more concerned with the question of human nature and therefore with the body-mind problem and its difficulties than the rest of philosophy and science. Psychological study necessarily involves the consideration of the relationship of the mind and the mental to the brain and bodily functions. The issue became so much more pressing when physiology in the nineteenth century presented facts which demanded an answer from psychologists. They were the findings about the brain, the functions of the brain, the localization of sensory functions in the brain, the dependence of speech on the brain, reflex activity, the nature of the nerve impulse, and the like, which were so closely related to what psychologists studied. Alexander Bain reflected the concern of psychology in 1872 when he said:

Many persons, mocking, ask—What has Mind to do with brain substance, white and grey? Can any facts or laws regarding the spirit of man be gained through a scrutiny of nerve fibers and nerve cells?

The question, whatever may be insinuated in putting it, is highly relevant, and raises great issues.

The issue of "connexion of mind and body," as Bain put it,

continued to be important even when the notion of the soul was not considered any more ("psychology without a soul"), and consciousness and mind were substituted for it. Later the mind was to be omitted, too, and only behavior left ("psychology out of its mind"). But as long as a distinction was being made between one series of events which were intangible and not directly observable, whether they were called psychic or mental, processes of consciousness or just psychological processes, and on the other hand, a series of bodily events, tangible and observable, still the issue of their relationship remained. It was considered the business and responsibility of psychology to explain this relationship and to tell us what is the "connexion" between the two classes of events. Of this responsibility psychologists were always aware and they tried to live up to it, especially the pioneers of the new psychology.

There were various formulations of the body-mind problem which psychologists usually adopted from philosophy. Among the early ones there was *Interactionism,* already known to us, which had followers until the nineteenth century. There was *Hylomorphism,* unpopular after Descartes, and although revived by Neoscholastic philosophy in the latter part of the nineteenth century, had little influence on the builders of scientific psychology. There was the *identity view* which postulated that the mind and the body are essentially identical, and the *double-aspect* theory which considered the mental and the bodily as merely two different aspects of the same thing. Later, after 1910, the Gestalt school introduced the doctrine of *Isomorphism* which saw a correspondence in spatial arrangement and structural order between the physical world, the senses, and the brain. However, the most popular and widely accepted doctrine of the psychology of the nineteenth century and of the new psychology when it originated as an independent science was *psychophysical parallelism.*

Fechner's Psychophysics.

Before we consider Psychophysical Parallelism, we must turn for a moment to a special brand of dualism, namely, the Psychophysics of Fechner. We mentioned Psychophysics and Fechner before, and here we merely wish to call attention to Fechner's idea about the relation of body and mind. Fechner was a philosopher and a physicist who occupied a place of prominence in the development of psychology because of his psychological investigations and the methods which he devised. His views on the body-mind relationship deserve our notice.

The relationship of body and mind, or more correctly, the soul, preoccupied Fechner throughout his entire life and is the central problem of his Psychophysics. The whole system of Psychophysics which Fechner developed and which he hoped to perfect revolved around the way the soul and the body are related to each other and the question of how we can know the soul through the body. For him there was no real difference between the spiritual and the material, indeed they were fundamentally identical. The distinction which is made between the spiritual and the material, or the mental and the bodily, is only a distinction between two aspects of the same reality. To explain what he meant Fechner used the analogy of the circle which appears concave from within and convex from without. All his efforts were directed toward the examination of the exact correspondence between the soul and the body, and the methods through which this correspondence could be studied. It was Fechner's methods which survived in psychology, not his philosophy. Psychophysics now refers not to the study of the relation between the body and the mind, but to the study of stimulus-response relationship.

The Meaning of Psychophysical Parallelism.

The germ of psychophysical parallelism was in the Leib-

57

nitzian parallelism. The first formulation of psychophysical parallelism and its direct application to psychology was probably made by Spencer in 1855 in his *Principles of Psychology*. However, the formulation which the new psychology of the late nineteenth century seized upon came from Alexander Bain (1818-1903) who took full cognizance of the problems which the young psychology had to face. It was implicit in his two capital books, *The Senses and the Intellect* (1855) and *The Emotions and the Will* (1859), but it was explicitly expounded in a separate book, *Mind and Body, The Theories of Their Relation* (1872). Bain, whom we mentioned before, and of whom we shall say more in later sections of the book, felt the need for a doctrine which would permit him to integrate the facts of anatomy and physiology with mental processes. The study of the brain, the physiology of the nervous system and of the sense organs, all contribute, in his opinion, to psychology, and psychology has to incorporate their findings. Psychophysical parallelism appeared to him the most suitable doctrine for psychology.

Psychophysical Parallelism assumes the existence of two realms, one spiritual or mental, the other material or physical. Between these two realms there is no causal relationship, yet the events in one are paralleled in the other realm. There are, in other words, two series of events which though independent are exactly parallel or coincide with each other in space and time. In man, then, every mental activity, such as perceiving or thinking, has its bodily counterpart and every bodily activity such as the brain process, has its counterpart in the mind without, however, one being the source or the cause of the other, and yet one could not occur without the other. Such a formulation implied that psychologists may study mental processes or consciousness and their neurophysiological parallels or correlates without being concerned at all about the philosophical problem of whether or how the mental and the bodily processes exert any effect upon each other. Relief from this concern was welcomed by dualistic psychologists. Especially physiological psychologists whose task it is to correlate physiological and psychological events (or psychic and physical) found comfort in Psychophysical Parallelism.

In his discussion of parallelism, Bain did not always make clear whether there was one or two substances in man. That is probably why some count him a dualist and others a monist. In the last paragraph of his *Mind and Body* he speaks of one substance and seems to think that he is close to Aristotle, but his solution of the body-mind relationship is certainly different from the Aristotelian Hylomorphism:

The arguments for the two substances have, we believe, now entirely lost their validity; they are no longer compatible with ascertained science and clear thinking. The one substance, with two sets of properties, two sides, the physical and the mental—a *double-faced unity*—would appear to comply with all the exigencies of the case. We are to deal with this, as in the language of the Athanasian Creed, not confounding the persons nor dividing the substance. The mind is destined to be a double study —to conjoin the mental philosopher with the physical philosopher; and the momentary glimpse of Aristotle is at last converted into a clear and steady vision.

This view was to be held by the majority of early psychologists.

Psychophysical Parallelism in Psychology.

That experimental psychologists were concerned with the merits of psychophysical parallelism is evidenced by the controversy around this issue at the Third International Congress of Psychology in Munich in 1896. Carl Stumpf, as co-president of the Congress delivering the inaugural address, used this occasion to discuss the respective merits of interactionism and parallelism. This opening address apparently imparted a tone to the whole Congress because throughout its duration the body-mind problem was vividly discussed. Stumpf strongly attacked Parallelism and favored Interactionism, and this was probably the last official defense of Interactionism by a psychologist. The majority of the 450 participants were decidedly on the side of Psychophysical Parallelism.

Psychophysical Parallelism appealed to the new psychology because it simplified matters for it, so to speak. As long as the existence of the two essentially different elements in man was presupposed—and this presupposition was almost universal—this parallelism was thought useful since it dispensed with the need of explaining the true nature of these two elements, the body and the soul, as well as the nature of their relationship. It could now be held that the soul and the body live their own lives, have their own businesses, and do not influence each other. The psychologist did not have to look into their mutual dealings at all. He was free to overlook the question of the spiritual and the material in man. It was then that the era of "psychology without a soul" was born.

The founder of psychology, *Wilhelm Wundt,* on psychophysical parallelism in his *Outlines of Psychology* (1896):

The principle that all those contents of experience which belong at the same time to the mediate or natural scientific sphere of treatment and to the immediate or psychological sphere, are related to each other in such a way that every elementary process on the psychical side has a corresponding elementary process on the physical side, is known as the *principle of psycho-physical parallelism*. It has an empirico-psychological significance and is thus totally different from certain metaphysical principles which have sometimes been designated by the same name, but which have in reality an entirely different meaning. These metaphysical principles are all based on the hypothesis of a psychical substance. They all seek to solve the problem of the interrelation of body and mind, either by assuming *two* real substances with attributes which are different, but parallel in their changes, or by assuming *one* substance with two distinct attributes which correspond in their modifications. In both these cases the metaphysical principle of parallelism is based on the assumption that every physical process has a corresponding psychical process and vice versa, or on the assumption that the mental world is a mirroring of the bodily world, or that the bodily world is an objective realization of the mental. This assumption is, however, entirely indemonstrable and leads in its psychological application to an intellectualism which is contradictory to all experience. The psychological principle of parallelism, on the other hand, as above formulated, starts with the assumption that there is only *one* experience, which, however, as soon as it becomes the subject of scientific analysis, is, in some of its components, open to *two* different kinds of scientific treatment, to a mediate form of treatment, which investigates ideated objects in their objective relations to one another, and to an *immediate* form, which investigates the same objects in their directly known character, and in their relations to all the other contents of the experience of the knowing subject.

Body-Mind Problem Today.

Psychophysical Parallelism was found to be a useful theoretical doctrine particularly by psychologists whose relations with the philosophy of the immediate past were still close and fresh. It was found a convenient device by those who wished to escape the perplexities of the body-mind relationship. In the final analysis, however, psychophysical parallelism could not satisfy all, neither completely nor for long. The reasons are rather obvious. To begin with, the doctrine represented a remnant from the philosophical heritage which psychology, in its striving for independence and scientific status, was eager to shake off or at least not to prolong. Psychologists did not wish to be beset by philosophical problems any more and thus were anxious to relegate theoretical issues of a philosophical nature to philosophy. The dichotomy of man, inherent in Psychophysical Parallelism, contained a suggestion of a possible essential difference between the mental and the bodily, a suggestion of the soul with all its theological implications which were to be avoided in the era of evolutionism. Moreover, the assumption of this dichotomy was contrary to the growing emphasis on the unity of man as an organism. Combine all these reasons with the rise of positivistic philosophy, the general progress of science, the theory of evolution, and, on the other hand, the decline of the influence of religion on modern thought, and the gradual and ultimate disappearance of Psychophysical Parallelism from psychology will be so much more understandable.

Despite the above reasons and the eventual disappearance of the doctrine of Psychophysical Parallelism, the body-mind issue has not disappeared from psychological discussions. Books and articles of recent origin attest to this fact. The issue has recurred with persistence, although not always in the same form, especially whenever basic theoretical problems of psychology are raised, or when specifically, the question of the physical and the psychological is disputed. Herbert Feigl in 1958 in his "The 'Mental' and the 'Physical' " notes: "But despite the considerably greater scientific and logical sophistication in recent treatments of the issue, it is somewhat depressing to note that the main philosophical positions still are these: materialism, mentalism, mind-body interactionism, evolutionary emergence theories, psychoneuro-physiological parallelism (epiphenomenalism, isomorphism, double aspect theories), and neutral monism."

Whatever view about man's nature may be adopted, or whatever philosophical or theological system followed by individual psychologists, the general conclusion which prevails in contemporary psychology is that man should be studied as a unitary biological organism without philosophical bias or prejudice, using for this study exclusively scientific data and methods.

SUMMARY

Scientific psychology at the time of its origin was dualistic, that is, it assumed that man is composed of two elements, the soul, or the mind, and the body. The first clear distinction of these two elements in man was made by Plato in the fourth century B.C. Dualism demanded an explanation of the relationship between the body and mind which created what has been called the body-mind problem. Various philosophical systems attempted to solve this problem in accordance with their basic views. Aristotle, also in the fourth century B.C., proposed one such solution, called the hylomorphic doctrine which was later followed and developed by Scholastic philosophy.

Psychology since the seventeenth century followed the dualism originated by Descartes. His was an extreme dualism which made man a composite of two substances of different natures, one of which was the material body, working like a machine, governed by the laws of physics, and the other one, the immaterial soul, endowed with rational intellect and free will, independent of the material world. Although there were monistic psychologies which departed from this division and postulated identity of both the psychic operations and the somatic processes, the general trend continued in the Cartesian tradition.

The distinction, if not always between the soul and the body, certainly between the mind and the body, or the mental and the bodily, or the physical, has continued, keeping the issue of their relation alive in psychology. The most widely accepted view as to the relationship between the mind and the body was the psychophysical parallelism which taught that the psychic and the bodily events occur in man in parallel fashion, that they coincide without being intrinsically dependent on each other. It was Alexander Bain in the latter part of the nineteenth century who formulated psychophysical parallelism and applied it to the whole of psychology. Psychophysical parallelism was the basic doctrine of the new scientific psychology and as a doctrine disappeared only in the later phase of psychology. The body-mind issue is, however, still discussed today.

4

Empirical Philosophy

The development of a new philosophy in the seventeenth century in England, known as empirical philosophy or empiricism, was of the utmost significance for psychology. This philosophy gave psychology its theoretical springboard, posed for it new problems and opened a new approach to their study. It was a source of psychology's scientific character and a contributing agent in psychology's emancipation. Other agents important in this emancipation, which we intend to take up later, like the interest in sensation and perception in philosophy, and Associationism, cannot be considered except in connection with empirical philosophy within which they grew and developed. Empirical philosophy made the association of ideas a very fundamental concept, and sensation and perception, because they were the principal sources of ideas, were its primary concern. We will first turn our attention to the empirical character of this new philosophical system, leaving the other aspects, sensationism and associationism, for discussion in the next two chapters.

The word empiric or empirical comes from the Greek word *empeirikos,* meaning "experimental," or *empeiria,* meaning "trial, attempt, experiment." Empirical is that which pertains to experience, or which pertains to the methods or results based on observation or experiment. It is opposed to rationalistic or deductive. Empirical philosophy was the name of the British philosophy developed by Hobbes, Locke, Berkeley, and Hume in the seventeenth and eighteenth centuries because this philosophy accepted experience, both external and internal, as the only valid source of knowledge. In this respect it differed from the rationalistic philosophy which relied chiefly on innate ideas, pure speculation without reference to experience, and on deduction. It was represented, for instance, by Descartes and Leibnitz. The latter, notwithstanding his respect for science and for the value of its methods, built his psychology on assumptions and *a priori* principles. Psychology as a science stems not from the rationalistic but from the empirical tradition.

Empirical Philosophers.

Thomas Hobbes (1588-1679) could be regarded as the first of the empirical philosophers, but it was *John Locke* (1632-1704) who was the real founder of the empirical philosophy for he laid the foundation of this system by insisting that experience is and should be the only means of attaining knowledge. He declared that "all the materials of reason and knowledge" come from experience, and that in experience "all our knowledge is founded and from that it ultimately derives itself." *George Berkeley* (1685-1753) in the same spirit studied man's mental world and its relation to the material world. His thesis, which is the main characteristic of his system, was that the material world is made or generated by the mind. "To be," he declared, "is to be perceived," which meant that a thing exists only insofar as it is perceived. This view made Berkeley the precursor of the philosophical school of Idealism which flourished in the nineteenth century. *David Hume* (1711-1776) probed more deeply and more critically than the other empiricists into the possibility and validity of knowledge through experience. The British Associationism of *James Mill, John*

Stuart Mill, and *Alexander Bain* was the continuation of this empirical philosophy. In France Empiricism was represented by *Etienne de Condillac* (1715-1780) and *Charles Bonnet* (1720-1793). The former was the most ardent exponent and propagator of Locke's views in France.

John Locke.

John Locke studied and practiced medicine for some time, but his main interest was directed to politics in which he was active for many years. Only when he was 58 years old did he become known as a philosopher after the publication of his principal philosophical work, *An Essay Concerning Human Understanding* (1690). It was the reading of Descartes' works which aroused Locke's interest in philosophy but the system which Locke subsequently built constituted the most powerful opposition to the Cartesian philosophy. He particularly opposed the Cartesian notion of innate ideas, arguing that the human mind is like a "white sheet," and that all the ideas of the human mind are acquired through personal experience. They are acquired either by the senses or through reflection which is a "perception of the operations of our own mind," as Locke described it. In the acquisition of knowledge, the mind plays a passive role of a receptacle or a compartment in which ideas are stored.

Locke concentrated on the analysis of the human mind. His whole philosophical system was evolved not from metaphysical principles but from psychological analysis. This analysis was carried out consistently and formed both the basis and core of his philosophy. Because it created a tradition which eventually matured into an experimental psychology, it has gained for him in some histories the title of "founder of experimental psychology."

67

Primary and Secondary Qualities.

Locke taught that the external objects which we perceive possess two kinds of qualities, the primary and the secondary. The primary or original qualities are inseparable from the object, that is, the object must possess them in order to exist and be itself. They are the qualities such as extension, number, shape, motion, or rest. The secondary qualities, on the other hand, do not have real existence in the object itself and are not inseparable from the object. They are subjective products of the mind expressing the effect which the objects bring upon the mind. To demonstrate this second kind of quality, Locke referred to a common experience: when one hand is left for some time in warm water, and the other in cold water, and then both are put into lukewarm water, the previously warmed hand feels cool, and the chilled hand feels warm. Another example was that of a colored cloth which seems of different colors if viewed in sunlight, shade, or lamplight respectively. The quality of warmth or cold or color is not a real quality of the object but the effect the object has on our mind. Sound and taste belong to the same category. Let it be noted here that Locke often referred, as in the case of the hands in the water or the cloth, to common personal experience, and frequently quoted either his own observations or those related by reliable people. He was known for his interest in people and things. He was curious and liked to observe and study.

Association of Ideas.

In Locke's philosophy the notion of "idea" occupied an important place as it did in the whole of modern British philosophy. The explanation as to what exactly constitutes "an idea" differed with various British philosophers. Locke spoke of idea first as "that term which . . . serves best to stand for whatsoever is the object of the understanding when a man thinks."

Later he defined it as "the immediate object of perception, thought, or understanding." All our ideas come from the senses or reflection and they are expressed by words like whiteness, hardness, sweetness, man, army, elephant, and the like. Our knowledge, according to Locke, is composed of ideas, simple and complex. Association of ideas, as Locke understood it, was just a simple combination of two or several ideas. It was not a well developed doctrine in his system, and it was presented only later in a special chapter entitled "Association of ideas" added to a new edition of the *Essay* (1700) after all the basic tenets of his philosophy had been already formulated. Association of ideas assumed greater importance in later British philosophy and attained its full development in John Stuart Mill and Alexander Bain. The latter found it a very useful concept for psychology and built his psychology on it.

John Locke, *An Essay Concerning Human Understanding*
Book II, Chap. 12

We have hitherto considered those ideas, in the reception whereof the mind is only passive, which are those simple ones received from sensation and reflection before mentioned, whereof the mind cannot make one to itself, nor have any idea which does not wholly consist of them.

* * *

As simple ideas are observed to exist in several combinations united together, so the mind has a power to consider several of them united together as one idea; and that not only as they are united in external objects, but as itself has joined them. Ideas thus made up of several simple ones put together I call *complex;* such as are beauty, gratitude, a man, an army, the universe; which, though complicated of various simple ideas or complex ideas made up of simple ones, yet are, when the mind pleases, considered each by itself as one entire thing, and signified by one name.

Locke's Dualism.

It should be mentioned that while Locke rejected many

points of the Cartesian doctrine, principally its "innate ideas," he did not oppose Cartesian dualism. Dualism of mind and matter is implicit in Locke's whole system. The soul to him was substantial and spiritual, and the body was material. In the work entitled *The Reasonableness of Christianity as Delivered in the Scriptures* (1695) Locke defended the fundamental principles of religion and ethics. As Locke remained a dualist, the other great empiricist, Berkeley, took a bold step toward monism, idealistic monism, when he denied that matter as such existed at all by itself, and affirmed mind as the only immediate reality. Hume, on the other hand, rejected the real existence of both, matter and spirit, and proclaimed consciousness as the sole reality. Consequently, he dealt only with the phenomena of consciousness. These two great philosophers of the empirical school will receive more attention in the later sections when we come to discuss sensation and perception, and associationism in philosophy.

Many of Locke's views were later revived by other philosophers and carried by them to their ultimate conclusions and applications in psychology, philosophy, ethics, religion, politics, and education. This was done sometimes in obvious violation of the Lockean spirit or in a form with which he could not have possibly agreed.

Contributions of Empirical Philosophy to Psychology.

Empirical philosophy affected psychology in a number of ways. First of all, it made experience the principal source of knowledge and the main method in the study of man. It also made the data of experience the chief object of psychological inquiry. In doing this, it brought psychology closer to the physical sciences and opened the door for experimentation in psychology. Secondly, by focusing attention on the senses, perception, and images, through which we are able to know and experience the external world, a fact so much emphasized by it, empirical philosophy provided psychology with a rich field for exploration. It is no wonder that scientific psychology in its initial phase was a psychology of sensation and perception. Thirdly, in the association of ideas, another product developed and handed down by empirical philosophy, the early psychology found temporarily the most useful theoretical principle for the understanding of the operations and the nature of mind.

Naturally, as psychology matured, it discovered processes and functions other than association, and association was gradually de-emphasized and lost its all-important position in psychology. Psychology also found new interests and extended to new fields. Sensation and perception then no longer claimed psychology's undivided attention. In the next two chapters, we shall see how sensation, perception, and association were treated by philosophy and how they were prepared for assimilation by psychology.

SUMMARY

Empirical psychology was founded by John Locke in the seventeenth century. This philosophy began a phase of philosophical thought which constituted an immediate preparation for psychology. Experience and its source, the senses, which empirical philosophy emphasized so strongly, and this philosophy's concentration on the understanding of human mind, directed psychology towards observation, experiment, the study of sensation and perception, and of other mental operations. The product of the empirical school, from the historical viewpoint most important for psychology, was associationism because it became the actual philosophical foundation of the new psychology.

5

Philosophical Study of Sensation and Perception

It was natural for philosophy to be interested in the sense organs and sensation from the very beginning of its existence, for it was recognized early that our contact with the world is possible only through the senses.

As early as *ca.* 530 B.C. there was a Greek physician, *Alcmaeon* of Croton, who studied the connections between sense organs and the brain, and who distinguished between sensation itself and its interpretation by the mind. In the fourth century B.C. there was a treatise *On Sense Perception and the Sensory Objects,* published by *Theophrastus* (372-287 B.C.), which was at the same time a critical survey of earlier investigations on sensation. *Aristotle* devoted much attention to sensation. He established the five-fold division of the senses, although he realized fully, it is worth noting, that there are more than five sensations. He raised the question whether touch, which includes such different pairs of opposites as moist and dry, hard and soft, hot and cold, should be considered a single sense or rather a composite of senses.

Sensationism

As the study of the senses progressed, certain fundamental distinctions began to be made: the objects stimulating the sense organs, the sense organs and their functions, the image of the object in the mind, the raw information about the object supplied by the senses to the mind, and the elaboration by the mind of this information or of the sensorial material received from the senses. The first significant contribution in this respect was made by the empirical philosophers of the seventeenth and eighteenth centuries who had a special reason for studying sensation. Empirical philosophy taught, as we already know, that all knowledge and all ideas come from the senses. The Cartesian notion of innate ideas was completely rejected by empiricism. The "tabula rasa" concept of the past, that is, that the mind in the beginning is like a blank or empty sheet, was resurrected by the empiricists although in a slightly different meaning. This concept and figure had been strongly advocated four centuries before by the Scholastics and was expressed in Thomas Aquinas' axiom: there cannot be anything in the intellect which was not previously in some form in the senses. But Descartes' influence ran contrary to this Scholastic stand, as it did in general against Scholasticism, and the "tabula rasa" idea was forgotten. Empirical philosophy returned to this concept, if not to the same term, and made the senses the main source of the knowledge about the external world. A large part of the empiricists' works was devoted to the discussion of the senses. Hobbes and Locke, Berkeley and Hume, and others of the empirical school wrote on sensation. The theory that sensation is the principal source of knowledge is called *sensationism*. It was the basic characteristic of empirical philosophy.

Reflection as a Source of Knowledge.

The senses, however, were not the only source of all experience or knowledge. If the mind is like "white paper," "void of all characters, without any ideas, how comes it to be furnished?," Locke asked. One source, or "fountain of knowledge," as Locke put it, we have just mentioned: the senses. But there is another fountain: reflection. "These two," that is, the senses and reflection, Locke says, "are the fountains of knowledge from whence all the ideas we have or can naturally have do spring."

While sensations furnish the ideas of objects outside ourselves, like their primary qualities, reflection is this mental operation which accounts for the ideas which do not come directly from the senses or can be traced to their operations. In Locke's definition, reflection is "the perception of the operations of our own mind within us, and it is employed about the ideas it has got." Reflection is not used by children who rely solely on their senses for the acquisition of knowledge about the world surrounding them. It comes later with maturity, but there may be men who never attain it, Locke said, and whose knowledge, therefore, remains on a lower level.

Berkeley's New Theory of Vision.

How strong the empiricists' preoccupation with sensation was and what role was assigned to reflection is well demonstrated in Berkeley's major work, *An Essay towards a New Theory of Vision* (1709). Berkeley selected vision for his discussion because this sense and its phenomena were best suited for the exposition of his philosophical principles. His plan was, as he stated at the beginning of the work, "to show the manner wherein we perceive by sight the distance, magnitude, and situation of objects: also to consider the difference there is betwixt the ideas of sight and touch, and whether there be any idea common to both senses." The main effort then of Berkeley's inquiry was directed toward the understanding of our knowledge of space, or in other words, to finding out how we come to know spatial relations. The immediate data of sight, Berkeley explained, are light and colors of objects, but the size, distance, and movement of objects are not the data of vision, but inductions based on internal experience. This internal experience arises from the eye muscles as they move the eyes in accordance with the position of the objects, either in motion or stationary, distant or near. This experience serves as a basis for induction about the movement, size, and distance of the objects. Knowledge of space, Berkeley concluded, is not the result of vision proper: "Space or distance," he said, "is no other wise the object of sight than of hearing."

The problem of space perception has been passed on from philosophers to psychologists, and has not ceased to interest modern psychologists. It is still the object of modern investigations and discussions, and to a great degree still remains unsolved. Like the psychologists of the preceding century, psychologists of the twentieth century not infrequently refer to Berkeley when they discuss space perception.

The conviction which Berkeley formed after his analysis of vision and of other senses was that even the qualities of the objects, called by Locke primary or original, like space, time, and movement, are products of the mind, similar to the secondary qualities. According to him, the external experience, obtained through the senses, was of lesser value in the acquisition of knowledge than the internal experience through reflection and ideas. One can see how such views logically led Berkeley toward Idealism.

Distinction between Sensation, Perception, and Image.

The sources of knowledge having been established and agreed upon by the philosophers of the empirical school, the next task for them was to analyze the products of sensations and mental operations, and to study how these products are related. As Locke and Berkeley paid attention principally to sensations and their role in experience. Hume himself concentrated on ideas. He was the first to discriminate clearly between what he called *impressions,* that is, the sensory data obtained by the mind through sensation, and their copies, *ideas,* preserved in memory and used in imagination. To quote Hume: "An impression first strikes upon the senses, and makes us perceive heat or cold, thirst or hunger, pleasure or pain of some kind or other. Of this impression there is a copy taken by the mind, . . . this we call an idea." The difference between them, Hume said, "consists in the degrees of force and liveliness with which they strike upon the mind, and make their way into our thought or consciousness." The meaning of Hume's idea corresponds to the meaning of image in the present psychological terminology. In his writings Hume listed and discussed the characteristics of impressions and ideas, and the differences existing between them.

The Scottish School.

The distinction between sensation and image was further clarified by *Thomas Reid* (1710-1796), otherwise an opponent of Hume's philosophy. He explained how sensory data are transformed into mental material and how they are true representations of external objects. Another significant distinction which Reid was able to make clearly was the distinction between sensation proper and perception. It is he who holds the honor of being the first in the history of psychology to differentiate and to attempt to define sensation and perception. He used the perception of the rose as an illustration of the differences between the two processes, an illustration often cited by subsequent psychological writers. All the senses received extensive treatment in Reid's works. He is credited with the introduction of the muscle sense into psychology. In general, Reid made sensation and perception the main topics of psychology.

Of interest also is the fact that it was Reid who advocated the notion of mental faculties or active powers of the mind.

Psychology built on this notion that the mind has distinct powers, independent of each other, came to be called "faculty psychology," which was vigorously opposed and largely discredited by modern psychologists. Reid's view that the mind is a composite of faculties was followed by the founder of phrenology, Franz Joseph Gall (1758-1828), who gave it a physiological flavor when he assigned sites in the brain to the various faculties.

Thomas Reid, *Essays on the Intellectual Powers of Man* Essay II, Chap. 5

In speaking of the impressions made on our organs in perception, we build upon facts borrowed from anatomy and physiology, for which we have the testimony of our senses. But, being now to speak of perception itself, which is solely an act of the mind, we must appeal to another authority. The operations of our minds are known, not by sense, but by consciousness, the authority of which is as certain and as irresistible as that of sense.

In order, however, to our having a distinct notion of any of the operations of our own minds, it is not enough that we be conscious of them; for all men have this consciousness. It is farther necessary that we attend to them while they are exerted, and reflect upon them with care, while they are recent and fresh in our memory. It is necessary that, by employing ourselves frequently in this way, we get the habit of this attention and reflection; and, therefore, for the proof of facts which I shall have occasion to mention upon this subject, I can only appeal to the reader's own thoughts, whether such facts are not agreeable to what he is conscious of in his own mind.

The philosophy of Reid was carried on and its influence further spread by his disciple, *Dugald Stewart* (1758-1828), professor at the Edinburgh University for 35 years, one of the greatest teachers of philosophy in British history. His collaborator for many years, *Thomas Brown* (1778-1820), departed from the orthodox Scottish school and approached associationism. He represents the transition from the Empirical school to Associationism. His extensive treatment of sensation and perception in his lectures on the *Philosophy of the Human Mind* (1820) should be pointed out here as another milestone of sensory philosophy. Other psychological problems, like emotions and a succession of mental states, likewise received his attention.

The Scottish school in general represents an opposition to certain dangerous, as they have been called, exaggerations of empirical philosophy, mostly to Hume's skepticism. It was a reaction of men who, recognizing the value of empirical method, did not want to be drawn too far, or to fall victims of materialism, and be robbed of notions such as the soul and conscience.

In the United States the Scottish tradition dominated psychology for the whole century before William James. Its last representatives were two professors of psychology (or of mental science, as psychology was then called in America), and presidents of two universities, Yale and Princeton, respectively: *Noah Porter* (1811-1882) and *James McCosh* (1818-1894). They were the last great exponents of the "old" psychology on American soil.

Sensationism in Other Countries

French Empiricism and French Materialism were notoriously sensationistic. Outstanding example of this trend in France is *Etienne de Condillac* (1715-1780). He began there the philosophical tradition which eventually effected the acceptance of the new psychology in that country. Brought up in British Empiricism, he carried the sensationistic doctrine to the extreme and made the senses and sensation the source of consciousness and all its phenomena. Mind was generated by sensations, he maintained, and illustrated this by the famous example of an inanimate marble statue. This statue becomes alive, and a thinking, feeling, and willing individual through sensations and sensory experience alone. Condillac's position and prestige were strong in France, and subsequent psychological writers always referred to him either in agreement and in effort to complement him, or in disagreement and with intention to refute him.

Sensationism was not strong in German philosophy, but the contributions of that country to sensory physiology were notable. Special notice is merited by *Hermann Lotze* (1817-1881) who, as philosopher and physiologist, studied sensation and space perception.

One could trace the philosophical interest and progress in sensation and perception further and quote more philosophers and systems. However, it is not important for us to make a complete record of these developments. The important thing is to note how strong this interest in philosophy was, how it reached its peak in empirical philosophy and British Associationism, and to realize that psychology inherited it from philosophy together with views on the whole subject of sensation and perception.

Sensory Physiology.

On the other hand, it must be noted also that philosophy on its own could neither encompass nor solve all the problems related to sensation and perception. The numerous scientific observations and investigations of sensory phenomena, especially visual, that were reported with increasing frequency from the middle of the eighteenth century could not but leave an impression on philosophy. The extensive work of 885 pages in 1759 by William Porterfield, *A Treatise on the Eye, the Manner and Phenomena of Vision,* can serve as a good example of the scientists' contribution to the problem of sensation. In the field of color vision there were observations of color phenomena by *Thomas Young,* around 1800, whose theory of color vision was improved some 60 years later by Helmholtz and is known as the Young-Helmholtz theory. Outstanding were the studies of the poet *Wolfgang Goethe.* In his *Zur Farbenlehre* ("On Colors") (1810), many new phenomena of color perception were described in detail. Many famous physiologists of the nineteenth century carried on systematic experimental work on the senses and sensations.

It became obvious to philosophers and to all concerned that physics, anatomy, physiology had to be consulted for information about sensory stimuli and sensory processes, the sense organs and their functions. Philosophical discussions without reference to scientific data could hardly hope for an adequate understanding of the human mind which, as philosophy raised in the empirical tradition taught, depended on sensation. The realization of this necessity was a factor in psychology's later separation from philosophy and closer union with physiology. Scientific psychology, when it was emancipated from philosophy, embraced both the philosophy of sensation, or speaking more broadly, the philosophy of cognition, and sensory physiology.

SUMMARY

Since the senses were the source of knowledge, as empirical philosophy taught, their study was essential. The interest in the senses was always present in philosophy, but empirical philosophers devoted particular attention to sensation and perception as the fundamental processes in the understanding of human mind. George Berkeley of the early eighteenth century, and his "new theory of vision," were quoted as an illustration of this trend within empirical philosophy. Thomas Reid in the same century made sensation and perception the main topics of psychology. His contributions to sensory psychology were significant. Beginning with the eighteenth century experimental studies of sensory functions and phenomena, especially visual, were undertaken and were soon followed by more precise studies of the sense organs and their functions by physiologists. Both the dissatisfaction with the results of the philosophical study and the appreciation of the rich fruit of physiological investigations in the field of sensation undoubtedly played part in psychology's emancipation from philosophy.

6

Associationism

Of all the philosophical systems it was the school of Associationism which exerted the strongest and most direct influence on psychology. Originated in Britain and developed by British philosophers, it was called British Associationism or the English school of Associationism. As a doctrine, Associationism represented the culmination of psychological thought within empirical philosophy. By the mid-nineteenth century it was ready to be used and absorbed by the new psychology, as being a doctrine best suited in the opinion of most pioneers of the new psychology for the explanation of the mind and its operations. E. G. Boring in his *History of Experimental Psychology* called Associationism "the substructure of the new physiological psychology." The reason for this appellation will be obvious after we have analyzed the meaning of Associationism and its development. Without studying Associationism, one could not fully understand the origin of scientific psychology or its early character.

We call Associationism that system which made the association of ideas the basic mental process. This process was to explain all the contents and phenomena of consciousness, and even as the associationists of the nineteenth century thought, the very nature of mind. Associationism grew out of empirical philosophy. Founded in the first half of the eighteenth century and fully developed in the next century, it was consistently

82

used and applied in the system of psychology of Alexander Bain (1818-1903). Its influence reached other countries and the founder of scientific psychology himself, Wilhelm Wundt.

The Meaning of Association.

The concept of association of ideas, although fostered and developed by empirical philosophy, was not its invention. Association of ideas is almost as old as philosophy. As soon as men began to analyze the human mind, they readily observed that thoughts come in succession, that one thought evokes another or that some thoughts always appear together. Moreover, it was noticed that certain events, if experienced at the same time or in succession, are consequently remembered together, and thus when one of these events is recalled the others also easily and promptly come to mind. We experience association of ideas when, for example, the thought of Christopher Columbus brings readily to our mind the discovery of America; when we see a cow, we think of milk; when we hear about New York's Broadway, we imagine its theatres and lights. Whenever one thought or idea evokes another, when two or more of them tend to appear in our mind together, or when the same external event is succeeded by the same sensation, we say that they are associated. The process or operation by which they are bound or linked together is called association. With the progress of philosophy, which further analyzed association, its meaning was broadened. The definition of the association of ideas which we find in J. M. Baldwin's *Dictionary of Philosophy and Psychology* is this: "A union more or less complete formed in and by the course of experience between the mental dispositions corresponding to two or more distinguishable contents of consciousness, and of such a nature that when one content recurs, the other content tends in some manner or degree to recur also."

The Use of Association in Philosophical Psychology.

When philosophy undertook to explain mental phenomena, the process of association was seized upon as a process useful for this purpose. Initially its application was limited to a single area, to memory. It was Aristotle who first explained memory in terms of association. He was especially successful in demonstrating the usefulness of association in the explanation of recall: one item can lead to the recall of another item if both these items are in some way associated, either because they are similar or opposites, or because they occurred at the same time or in the same place. The linking of two or more items was seen by Aristotle to follow certain laws which he defined and discussed. They were the first laws of association. Aristotle, and after him many others, particularly the great Associationists of the eighteenth and nineteenth centuries, tried to explain by such laws the reasons why ideas are linked together or become associated. Various laws were suggested but the most persistent one, reiterated by many philosophers, was the law of contiguity. It meant that events or ideas contiguous in time or space, that is, occurring either simultaneously or successively, or in the same place, tend to become associated in the mind and thus are apt to recur together.

The process of association was utilized in a practical way in mnemotechnics or methods of memorizing. To illustrate this, let us give two examples. The battle at Zama during the Punic war was fought in 202 B.C. It will be easy to remember this date if one associates it with the exclamation, well-known to the student of history, of the Carthaginian general, Hannibal, who was defeated at Zama: "Zama, O Zama." Since Z resembles 2, one can easily connect the first letters of this exclamation into 202. This way the very name of the battle place helps to recall the date. Another example of mnemotechnics is the word *HOMES* which helps to recall the names of the Great Lakes in the United States because its letters stand for these names, *H* for Huron, *O* for Ontario, and so on.

A systematic application of association not only to memory but to other aspects of mind had to wait until the arrival of empiricism. It was the empirical school that used association for the explanation of knowledge and introduced the term *association of ideas.* Association then began to be employed to the best advantage of empirical philosophy, which took upon itself the task of explaining the acquisition of knowledge, and to be extended by it from memory to other mental processes, cognitive as well as affective. Finally it became in British Associationism the basic psychological principle applied to all mental life. The most complex mental processes, indeed the nature of mind, were explained by association.

The application of association was extended in still another direction. Physiologically minded Associationists, of whom D. Hartley is an example, made use of association in accounting for the functioning of the brain, thus referring association to physical processes as well. Moreover, association was believed to exist between functions of the sense organs together with the corresponding neural events in the brain, on one hand, and sensations and other mental operations on the other hand. A parallel was thus thought to exist between the bodily and mental events. For some philosophers the neural events, associated with corresponding mental acts, constituted merely a physical substrate of these acts, whereas others saw a causal relationship between the neural and the mental, and some even thought them to be identical in nature. These tendencies appeared in Britain, in France, and elsewhere. Their bearing on the attempted solutions of the body-mind problem is obvious. The finding of correlates between the mental and the physiological was one of the primary objectives of the nineteenth century physiological psychology. This objective was reflected in the experiments at the Leipzig laboratory, and other laboratories which aimed at establishing the physiological reactions normally accompanying psychological experience in emotions.

The Associationistic Program.

The lines along which British Associationism proceeded can be briefly summarized in a few points. British Associationism sought: 1) to find and formulate the laws of association; 2) to analyze all facts of conscious life and demonstrate how they can all be explained by the associative process; 3) to break down the complex material of the conscious mind into the simplest elements possible; 4) to refer mental phenomena to the facts of anatomy and physiology, and to any other pertinent science; and finally, 5) to apply association and the empirical findings of Associationism to other branches of human knowledge and to build upon them the systems of ethics, logic, epistemology, jurisprudence, sociology, esthetics, and education.

British Associationists.

In this section we shall list the principal representatives of the Associationistic movement in Great Britain and their main contributions. The ancient concept of association, handed down by various philosophers, was modernized by *Thomas Hobbes* (1588-1679). It was subsequently discussed by *Locke* who was the first to use the term "association of ideas," and by *Berkeley*, but only *Hume* gave it full formulation within empirical philosophy. It was, however, *David Hartley* (1705-1757) who made association a consistent systematic principle and the core of his philosophy. He is the true founder of the school of Associationism. *Thomas Brown* (1778-1820) of the Scottish school used association in his psychology and developed it further. He called association by another name, *suggestion,* which meant the same thing. To the primary laws of association Brown added several new laws which he called the secondary laws. The culmination of British Associationism was reached in the nineteenth century in *James Mill* (1773-1836) and his son *John Stuart Mill* (1806-1873), whereas *Alexander Bain* in the second half of the nineteenth century marks the transition from association psychology, treated as part of philosophy, to independent scientific psychology. We shall now mention some of the highlights of this development of Associationism from Hume to Bain.

Association in Hume's Philosophy.

Association was discussed by Locke and Berkeley who preceded David Hume (1711-1776), but it was the latter who devoted more attention to it and treated it more thoroughly. His main philosophical works were the *Treatise of Human Nature* (1739-1740), and *An Inquiry Concerning Human Understanding* (1748). He doubted the reality of both the mind and the body, accepting only consciousness and its phenomena as the object of his inquiry. We have already seen (p. 176, *supra*) how Hume understood the distinction between sensation and perception (in his terminology collectively called "impression") and how he differentiated from them and their copy, the image (his "idea"). Ideas in Hume's understanding are preserved either in memory, where they remain unchanged and resemble closely the original impressions from which they originated, or in imagination where they may be altered. There were no other sources of knowledge than impressions and ideas. Locke's reflection as another source was not accepted by Hume.

Hume taught that ideas may be simple or complex, and both kinds may cohere in forming ideas. This coherence, combination, or association, of ideas is due to various factors. Among them, three are prominent: resemblance, contiguity in time or place, and cause and effect—the laws of association. The Associationists who succeeded Hume analyzed these laws further and looked for others. They also had another objective in mind, namely, to determine which ideas are simple, that is, a mere reproduction of some aspect of an external object, and those which are complex, or a combination of several simple ideas. A complex idea can be analyzed or be broken into its constituents or elements of simple ideas. The latter task became characteristic of the "mental chemistry" of the early scientific psychology. But Hume was not preoccupied with this, he merely formulated the concept of complex ideas as did Locke before him.

We should also add that association as Hume understood it was not simply a static constitution or an aggregate of simple ideas. It possessed the character of an act or process. This aspect was further accentuated in Hartley's discussion of association.

David Hartley, Founder of Associationism.

By profession a practicing physician, and a philosopher only by avocation, David Hartley (1705-1757) published in 1749, an important philosophical book, *Observations on Man,* the product of his work and thinking over a period of sixteen years. The originality and freshness of Hartley lay in his vigorous attempt to include and integrate both the facts of anatomy and physiology with the ideas of philosophy. On one hand he made use of anatomy as it was known in his day, and on the other hand, he applied Newton's physics, especially the latter's *vibratory action,* to the explanation of nervous activity. Newton's teaching was that light consists of vibrations of particles and the sensation of colors is the result of vibrations of different frequencies impinging upon the retina of the eye.

88

Hartley extended this concept of vibrations to all senses and to the nervous system.

He was the first to abandon completely the then prevalent notion of animal spirits residing in the brain and moving along the nerves which were thought to be hollow tubes. For him the brain, the spinal cord, and the nerves contained small (called by Hartley: "infinitesimal") particles which could be set in longitudinal motion. Sensations are the result of small vibrations in the nerves, whereas images and ideas, mental phenomena of the higher order, consist of still smaller and more delicate vibrations ("vibratiuncles") in the brain. The vibrations in the brain are the effect and the replica of the vibrations in the nerves. This correspondence between these two sets of vibrations is the reason why images and ideas are similar to the original sensations. Seeing a tree is one set of vibrations and having a mental image of a tree is another set of vibrations, but because these two sets of vibrations are correlated, the image of a tree is a faithful copy of the sensation of a tree. Hartley taught that if sensations and their accompanying vibrations are repeated often, they leave vestiges or traces in the nervous system. They are the simple ideas, and these coalesce into patterns and form complex ideas. Between the oft-repeated sensations, between them and their corresponding ideas, a strong bond is established so that any one sensation may evoke all ideas originally associated with it. This bond is again explained in physiological terms consistently with Hartley's associationistic views. It is simply a matter of permanent traces left by different sensations in different regions of the brain, and of nerve connections between these regions. Hence once such connections are established, vibrations started in one part of the brain easily revive vibrations in the other parts, thereby awakening ideas associated with them.

David Hartley, *Observations on Man,* Part I, Chap. 1

My chief design in the following chapter is briefly to explain, establish, and apply the doctrines of *vibrations* and *association*. The first of these doctrines is taken from the hints concerning the performance of sensation and motion, which Sir Isaac Newton has given at the end of his Principia, and in the Questions annexed to his Optics; the last, from what Mr. Locke, and other ingenious persons since his time, have delivered concerning the influence of *association* over our opinions and affections, and its use in explaining those things in an accurate and precise way, which are commonly referred to the power of habit and custom, is a general and indeterminate one.

The doctrine of *vibrations* may appear at first sight to have no connexion with that of association; however, if these doctrines be found in fact to contain the laws of the bodily and mental powers respectively, they must be related to each other, since the body and mind are. One may expect, that *vibrations* should infer *association* as their effect, and *association* point to *vibrations* as its cause. I will endeavour, in the present chapter, to trace out this mutual relation.

Hartley, the First Physiological Psychologist.

The idea of vibrating particles is obsolete now, although it was original and progressive then, but the paralleling of physiological and mental events, and the search for physiological counterparts or substrata of mental processes, as well as the localization of mental functions in the brain, have become the primary objective of physiological psychology. One may thus rightly call Hartley a physiological psychologist and his psychological system a system of Physiological Psychology. It was, if not the first altogether, the first British Physiological Psychology.

One would be inclined, on account of his explanation of mental phenomena in terms of vibrations of material particles, to think of Hartley as a materialistic psychologist like some of his contemporaries, de La Mettrie for example, who renounced the idea of a spiritual element in man and did not see any other explanation of mind but mechanical action of the nervous system. Yet Hartley was not a materialist. On the contrary, he insisted on being a spiritualist and strongly affirmed the existence of the immaterial and immortal soul in man different in nature from the body. The endeavor to bridge physiology with psychology, and to reconcile science with spiritual philosophy and religious beliefs is quite characteristic of Hartley and makes him an early champion of harmony between science, philosophy, and religion at the time when science had just begun to develop and Empirical Philosophy approached its peak. However, to psychology, historically speaking, he was not important on that account but rather for his Associationism and for the influence it exerted on the subsequent development of psychology.

Consistent Application of Association to all Psychology.

The whole Hartleyan interpretation of association would perhaps not have assumed in itself much importance were it not for the consistent application of association by Hartley to various psychological matters. Perception, emotion, language, memory, recall, imagination—all were explained by him in terms of association. Emotions, for instance, are experiences of pleasure or pain habitually associated with certain sensations, and memory is simply an accurate association. One can readily see how in Hartley's system association became an important psychological principle. Hartley made this principle much clearer than other philosophers had and he demonstrated in a convincing manner its usefulness for psychology, and its potentiality as the fundamental psychological law. Other associationists who came after Hartley picked up the problem where he left it and tried to develop the laws of association further and to find additional applications of association. Learning in later psychology, for example, will be the field where association will be used most extensively. The immediate successors of Hartley in Associationism were James and John Stuart Mill. Then came Bain who built his system of psychology on association. The final absorption of the Associationist tradition by scientific psychology was achieved by Wundt and his school. Let us see now how the two Mills developed the doctrine of association within their philosophies.

David Hartley, *Observations on Man,* Part I, Introduction

Man consists of two parts, body and mind.

The first is subjected to our senses and inquiries, in the same manner as the other parts of the external material world.

The last is that substance, agent, principle, etc., to which we refer the sensations, ideas, pleasures, pains, and voluntary motions.

Sensations are those internal feelings of the mind, which arise from the impressions made by external objects upon the several parts of our bodies.

All our other internal feelings may be called *ideas.* Some of these appear to spring up in the mind of themselves, some are suggested by words, others arise in other ways. Many writers comprehend *sensations* under *ideas*: but I every where use these words in the senses here ascribed to them.

The ideas which resemble sensations, are called *ideas of sensation*: all the rest may therefore be called *intellectual ideas.*

James Mill and his Mental Mechanics.

The two Mills, the father, James Mill (1773-1836), and his son, John Stuart Mill (1806-1873), mark the culmination of the British Associationism. The former was a historian and a political writer rather than a philosopher although philosophy and especially psychological problems strongly attracted him.

He was quite confident, too, about his ability in this respect because even long before he had any intention of writing a psychological book he said: "If I had the time to write a book, I would make the human mind as plain as the road from Charing Cross to St. Paul's." Later he did write his *Analysis of the Phenomena of the Human Mind* (1829), in which he sought to make the human mind plain indeed by treating it as a sort of machine and by simplifying it through association applied with utmost consistency to all mental phenomena. His was the first complete system of psychology constructed on this doctrine alone. The mind, which is like a blank sheet at birth, records all the experiences received through the senses. Sensations and their copies, ideas, may occur simultaneously or in succession. They are bound together into complex ideas by association whose function is merely to bind, and not to transform or modify anything in them. Thus complex ideas, the result of the associative process, contain all the single elements which entered into their formation without any change. The sensation of white is given by Mill as an analogy. He says in the *Analysis of the Phenomena of the Human Mind:*

Where two or more ideas have been often repeated together, and the association has become very strong, they sometimes spring up in such close combinations as not to be distinguishable. Some cases of sensation are analogous. For example, when a wheel, on the seven parts of which the seven prismatic colours are respectively painted, is made to revolve rapidly, it appears not of seven colours, but of one uniform colour, white. By the rapidity of the succession, the several sensations cease to be distinguishable; they run, as it were, together, and a new sensation, compounded of all seven, but *apparently* a simple one, is the result. Ideas, also, which have been so often conjoined, that whenever one exists in the mind, the others immediately exist along with it, seem to run into one another, to coalesce, as it were, and out of many to form one idea;

93

which idea however is in reality complex, *appears* to be no less simple, than any one of those of which it is compounded. *(Italics are ours)*

Note in this excerpt the words *appears* and *apparently* which we italicized. White, which—as we say in psychology now— *is* a simple sensation, to Mill only *appears* simple because, as he understands the operation of association, all the elements which make this sensation of white, the spectral colors, and similarly elements of any other sensations or ideas for that matter, still exist intact. Such a concept, according to which all the elements exist without any transformation in mental states made up by them, and remain in their original form, has been called *mental mechanics.* This mental mechanics is the distinctive characteristic of Mill's system, and it was this very aspect which John Stuart Mill set out to correct in his father's system.

John Stuart Mill and his Mental Chemistry.

James Mill's son, John Stuart Mill, represents what has been termed *mental chemistry.* Primarily a logician, author of *Logic* (1843), his most original work, he reworked his father's system by applying to it his own kind of associationism without repeating the whole analysis of the mind. He made this substitution in the notes which he added to his edition of his father's *Analysis of the Human Mind* (1869). His understanding of association can be illustrated by referring to his interpretation of the same sensation of white as it is presented in his *Logic*:

When impressions have been so often experienced in conjunction, that each of them calls up readily and instantaneously the ideas of the whole group, those ideas sometimes melt and coalesce into one another, and appear not several ideas but one; in the same manner as when the seven prismatic colors are presented to the eye in rapid succession, the sensation produced is that of white.

But in this last case it is correct to say that the seven colors when they rapidly follow one another *generate* white, but not that they actually are *white*; so it appears to me that the Complex Idea, formed by the blending together of several simpler ones, should, when it really appears simple, (that is, when the separate elements are not consciously distinguishable in it) be said to *result from*, or be *generated by*, the simple ideas, not to consist of them ... These are cases of *mental chemistry*: in which it is possible to say that these simple ideas *generate*, rather than that they compose, the complex ones. *(Italics are ours)*

Association, according to John S. Mill's view, is not a simple combination of elements, analogous to, let us say, a mixture of coffee and milk, but it is like a chemical process by which something completely different is made, analogous to water in which the characteristics of oxygen and hydrogen are completely lost. That is why he used the word *generate*: the complex idea is generated by simple ideas. The italicized expressions in the excerpt above show well the contrast between the two kinds of association, that of Mill the father and that of Mill the son, and also the novel characteristics of the latter's associationistic concept.

It will be well to keep the concept of mental chemistry in mind because scientific psychology will follow this approach at first. In its initial phase the new psychology was literally a chemistry of the mind, that is, it treated mind and its states like a chemical substance, and proceeded to find all its constituents and the mode of their connection. No doubt the science of chemistry which originated at the end of the eighteenth century and subsequently made fast strides, gave the impulse to such a conception. The first to use the idea of mental chemistry before John Mill was Thomas Brown who wrote in his *Lectures on the Philosophy of the Human Mind* (1820):

95

As in chemistry it often happens that the qualities of the separate ingredients of a compound body are not recognizable by us in the apparently different qualities of the compound itself—so, in this spontaneous *chemistry of the mind,* the compound sentiment that results from the association of former feelings has in many cases . . . little resemblance to these constituents.

The idea of mental chemistry was developed fully by J. S. Mill and applied by him to the whole range of mental phenomena where association was thought to operate. This was the brand of mental chemistry which was assimilated by the young science of psychology.

The Psychological System of Bain.

We have already met Alexander Bain (1818-1903) when we spoke of his psychophysical parallelism. Bain closes the prescientific period of psychology and opens the new era of scientific psychology. In this function he is similar to Germany's Herbart and Lotze who too represented the transition from philosophical to scientific psychology in their country. In Bain Associationism reaches its climax. Association as a psychological principle is extended by him to new problems of psychology like movement, habit, and will which were not treated to any extent by his predecessors. Indeed his whole system of psychology is built on this principle.

The greatest single contribution to psychology was Bain's large systematic *The Senses and the Intellect* (1855) and *The Emotions and the Will* (1859), abridged in 1868 as *Mental and Moral Science.* For almost fifty years this was the textbook of psychology in Britain, and it had a marked influence on American psychologists, including William James. The characteristics of this work, which signals the approaching scientific psychology, are the inclusion of physiological material (nervous system), the effort to integrate physiology with psychology, and the emphasis on the senses which, from now on, will characterize most of the early textbooks of psychology. In it we also see the second British attempt after Hartley to construct a physiological psychology, this time actually on discovered facts of anatomy and physiology and not merely on analogies. The book in its early editions did not treat of evolution. Later Bain gave an exposition of the evolutionary theory but did not weave it into his system.

We have to note another contribution of Bain: the founding of the periodical *Mind* (1876) which was the first psychological journal in the world. But *Mind* printed more philosophical than psychological articles and noticeably few experimental studies, unlike Wundt's *Philosophische Studien* (later transformed into *Psychologische Studien*) which, as a publication specifically devoted to reporting on investigations executed in his laboratory, contained a great deal of experimental material.

The First Experiment with Association.

Thus far, we have traced the development of associationistic thought, and it is to be noted at this point that all the philosophical views on association and its operation were either armchair speculations or, at best, the results of personal observations, but they were never submitted to experimental verification. One of the first things the new psychology undertook was to subject association to experimentation.

The experimental approach to association was initiated by *Francis Galton* around 1879. In this first experiment on association he presented seventy-five stimulus words and recorded the ideas (expressed in words) that were spontaneously elicited by them. He also measured the time between the stimulus word and the response word. That was the free association experiment, free because the subject in the experiment was at liberty to form any association and was to report the first idea that came to his mind. In this first experiment Galton himself was a subject. It inspired a series of experiments at the Leipzig laboratory, conducted with refined techniques. *James McKeen Cattell,* an American student of Wundt and the first American to obtain the doctorate in the new psychology there (1886), improved the experiment methodologically and technically, introducing an electric voice key to measure the associative reaction time, that is, the time between the presentation of the stimulus word and the response word. May we note in this respect that what Cattell, the American, did for experimentation on reaction time in applying better rigorous scientific controls, was symptomatic of what American psychology in general was to do for all psychology, namely, making it more rigidly experimental and improving its scientific methodology.

Opposition to Associationism.

As powerful as Associationism was, it did not win all minds. There was a current of philosophical thought which ran counter to Associationism as a philosophical school and against association as a basic psychological principle, and this opposition was not without profound effects on psychology. In fact, the hostile reaction to Associationist doctrine gained strength soon after the turn of the century and gave origin to an entirely different orientation in psychology.

Early opposition to Associationism, it will be remembered, came from the Scottish school, especially from Thomas Reid. He opposed the very basis of Associationism, that is, the ideas as they were presented and interpreted by Hume. The Scottish school had many followers in other countries. In the United States it was the most powerful single school before William James. The Idealistic philosophy of the nineteenth century, stressing the unity of the mind, created another opposition to

Associationism. Later, within the new psychology, Associationism met criticism from Brentano and his disciples (Act Psychology). James showed his reaction against the British school by vigorously denying that mind is a storehouse of images and ideas, or that it consists of operations or faculties, and instead presented it as a constant change, a stream of consciousness. For similar reasons also, Bergson rejected Associationism, objecting strongly to its atomizing of the mind. Gestalt psychology, whose origin was the result of the rebellion against the elementism of Associationism, fought it with this latter school's own weapon, perception, and emphasized the importance of the whole instead of elements in perception and in other processes.

The Effect of Associationism on Scientific Psychology.

In evaluating now the final effect of the varied development within Associationism on scientific psychology, we must point out that Associationism resulted in an *atomistic view of human mind and of behavior,* when the latter became the subject matter of psychology and was regarded as the sum of stimulus-response bonds. Atomizing was a general tendency of the nineteenth-century science and psychology followed this same trend. Biology discovered that living tissue is composed of cells, physics found matter to be built of atoms, chemistry succeeded in analyzing substances into elements and spoke of atoms and molecules, and medicine had its "atoms" of disease, the bacterium and the virus. And so psychology too, faithful to its Associationistic tradition, found the atoms of the mind, or in the terminology of the Associationist psychologists, the elements, of which all the states of consciousness were composed. The mind was interpreted as merely the sum of these elements which had to be found and analyzed. This was the prevailing view of the new psychology. This was the tenet of the Associationistic psychology, a true descendant of Associationistic philosophy, represented in Germany by Wilhelm Wundt and in America by E. B. Titchener, the leader of the school of Structuralism.

The principle of association was *extensively employed in the study of memory, learning, and conditioning.* The Behavioristic school presented an Associationistic explanation of behavior. The old laws of association, applied originally only to mental operations, were transformed by this school into laws of behavior and were invoked to *explain the stimulus-response relationship.* The Psychoanalytic school, especially Freudianism, can be called the latest transformation of Associationism applied to clinical psychology. For this school emphasized association between certain clinical manifestations and early life experiences, and employed free association technique in clinical examination of the patient.

Association as a basic theoretical doctrine of psychology was subsequently attacked and rejected by these psychological orientations which proclaimed and defended not mental atomism but *unity, integration, and wholeness* as the mind's true and essential characteristics. The arguments which they marshalled against Associationism and in support of their thesis were successful enough to discredit and eventually banish the "brick and mortar psychology" of Associationism. Today there is neither Associationistic philosophy nor Associationistic psychology. Some psychologists may still continue to overemphasize association and build their psychology around this process, but in general, present-day psychologists agree that association is not *the* process but only *a* process among many psychological processes. The former pretentiousness of association as the basic principle in psychology has yielded to the much more modest role of a process of association.

SUMMARY

Association as a psychological process was studied and discussed in philosophy since Aristotle. Empirical psychology made it a central function by which it attempted to explain knowledge. Association of ideas, first defined by Locke, assumed an ever-increasing importance in psychology. British Associationism, founded by D. Hartley, made use of association of ideas in many areas of psychology. James Mill and John Stuart Mill crystallized the principles of Associationistic psychology. A. Bain presented a whole system of psychology built on Associationism. Associationism served as the theoretical foundation of scientific psychology and gave it its original character. It was the first psychological doctrine. It was embraced by the school of Structuralism and Behaviorism. In its subsequent development psychology ceased to be merely associationistic psychology.

7

Philosophical Influences on Psychology in the Nineteenth Century

Thus far we have been preoccupied with the main fountains of psychological thought. We considered the systems, problems, and concepts within philosophy which played the most significant role in the origin and character of psychology as an independent science. They included the doctrine of Dualism and the body-mind problem, Empirical Philosophy, the philosophical study of sensation and perception, and the school of Associationism. While they constitute the most significant philosophical influences, there were, it must be realized, superimposed on this main philosophical stream many other influences and currents of thought of consequence for psychology. Some were only of minor consequence for the future of psychology as they were of brief duration or were represented by only a small group of psychologists. There were others, however, which left a more lasting imprint or affected larger groups of psychologists, changing the course of psychology in some particular respect, if not always of psychology in general, at least of psychology in one country. More specifically, these philosophical influences may have had an effect in one or in all of the following respects: 1) the subject matter, 2) methodology, 3) choice or emphasis on certain areas of research, 4) interpretation of experimental findings, and 5) psychological theory. Some of these effects have been salutary for psychology, others have been unfavorable and hindered psychology's progress.

Philosophy and Psychological Schools.

There was a period in the history of psychology (about 1910-1930) during which there were many psychologies rather than a single psychology. One American textbook of the history of psychology was even entitled *Seven Psychologies* (E. Heidbreder, 1933), and there were two volumes published here by C. Murchison bearing the respective titles *Psychologies of 1925* and *Psychologies of 1930*. The main reason for the emergence of psychological schools, or as we may say, different psychologies, was the difference in philosophies from which their basic theories were derived. For every school in psychology assumed particular doctrines which can be traced to some philosophical system. When we look into the theoretical assumptions of such schools as the Gestalt, Behaviorism, Psychoanalysis, or any other school, upon careful scrutiny we can detect their philosophical ancestry. Their dependence upon philosophy may not always be immediately apparent or recognized even by the founders of the schools, but, whether this dependence was subtle or unconscious, a thorough examination of the school's tenets usually reveals some kind of philosophical influence. If we survey the existing psychological schools of the past we discover that the Gestalt school was much indebted to the Austrian school (Act Psychology), and the doctrine of form-qualities of Christian von Ehrenfels. Behaviorism is a progeny of mechanistic philosophy and of the Positivism of the nineteenth century. The concept of the unconscious in the Psychoanalytical school was not a totally new idea, as it had its precursors in J. F. Herbart and E. von Hartmann. Similarly, the doctrines of other schools can be traced or related to the philosophies of the past. Almost invariably all the theories which we encounter in scientific psychology now can also be referred to some philosophical theories.

The undeniable fact is that philosophies did and always will affect psychology and psychologists as they did affect other sciences and human thought in general. Their influence extends not only to the thought alone, to the theory, but indirectly to life and practice as well. Often today's idea becomes tomorrow's action, and today's philosophical system takes flesh in tomorrow's social or political movement. "There is a lot of other people's work in everything we do," was the observation of Pascal. Nevertheless, it should be noted again, the influence of philosophy on human thinking and behavior may often be quite imperceptible. It may take its effect without awareness of the people who succumb to it. The medium of this influence may not be necessarily the printed work or spoken word, but frequently the atmosphere or spirit of the time bred by the given philosophical system. All these things are well known, but we feel that after having reviewed the major philosophical roots, it is appropriate to remind the student of the above possibilities before we make a survey of the nineteenth-century philosophical influences.

In this survey we shall mention the philosophers and philosophies whose impact on psychology had been noticeable and recognized by the historians of psychology. They all belong to the nineteenth century except for Immanuel Kant whose activity falls in the last two decades of the eighteenth century. Their influence in most cases showed its effect in nineteenth century psychology but in some cases it did not reach psychology until the twentieth century. We must be brief and cursory in our exposition and merely state the more obvious contributions or effects, particularly those of historical importance for psychology. Here is the list of those whom we will mention: in *Germany,* Kant, Herbart, and Lotze; in *Austria,* Mach; in

England, Spencer; and in *France,* Bergson. Special attention will be devoted to the school of Positivism. Neoscholastic philosophy, and Marxism with its effect on the psychology of Soviet Russia, will also be mentioned.

Immanuel Kant (1724-1804).

Fame came to Kant late in life, when he published his *Critique of Pure Reason* in 1781 at 57 years of age. He is one of the greatest philosophers in the history of human thought. He is great because he built a powerful synthesis in which he attempted to integrate the philosophical insights developed by rationalism and empiricism. As each of these trends had developed the logic of their opposing points of view, one stressing rational principles, the other the concrete; each begot a position which excluded and negated the other. Kant insisted that both views expressed a fundamental aspect of true science. His problem was how to justify both aspects at the same time. In doing so, as against Rationalism and its intuitive knowledge of the nature of things, he emphasized the limitations of human reason; as against Empiricism and its atomistic view of experience, he emphasized the synthesizing power of reason. His influence was profound and was felt in many different spheres of human thought, and Germany felt it more directly than other countries.

Kant is important in the development of the science of psychology because he applied his general critique of science to psychology. In the *Critique of Pure Reason* he showed that the content of our knowledge is from experience and so all empirical psychological data are important. But our awareness is limited to what appears or manifests itself. In accord with his critique we can know nothing of the nature of the soul as *noumenon,* or thing-in-itself. Beyond the mere data of appearances he notes that a science of these psychological phe-

105

nomena demands, as a condition of its very possibility as a science, a manner of synthesizing the data. These synthetic forms he likens to the logical structure of judgments, as, for example, the subject-predicate relation. The science of psychology was thus seen as a body of necessary judgments, the necessity stemming from the mental *a priori* forms synthesizing the observed psychic phenomena which were already given as linked by the internal temporal patterns of our sense experience. Empirical psychology deals with the data of our inner experience. Rational psychology as the supposed development of an understanding of the nature of the soul through its activity of thinking is beyond the power of human reason. Kant thus eliminates rational psychology from the realm of the sciences, philosophical or empirical. At the same time he ties his empirical psychology to the philosophical supposition of his necessary *a priori* conditions of knowledge.

The effects of Kantian philosophy on psychology are apparent in a number of ways: 1) This philosophy tempered the influence of Associationism in its emphasis on the *a priori* synthesizing forms of our consciousness. 2) It stresses that mind as consciousness or internal experience is the sole legitimate object of psychological inquiry. These data are resolved neither into physiological processes nor ontological natures or operations. 3) Introspection was stressed as a natural and respectable method. 4) By denying knowledge of the nature of thought or of extension, it attempted a union of the manifestations of both on the empirical level. 5) Nativism in psychology was to a degree reinforced through the *a priori* synthesizing forms. This Nativism was later represented by E. Hering, Stumpf, and the Gestalt school, and is still alive in contemporary psychology. 6) In general, Kantian philosophy brought succor to those who resisted the tendency to reduce mind to mere brain processes and to make psychology a chapter of physiology by providing them with a new and forceful philosophical doctrine.

Johann Friedrich Herbart (1776-1841).

We have already talked about Herbart in connection with the Leibnitzian apperception. He succeeded Kant in the chair of philosophy at Königsberg, but his philosophy was not a continuation of Kant's philosophy. It was a new and different system and if Herbart borrowed any ideas from other sources, it was not from Kant but rather from Leibnitz. His interest in psychology was much livelier and his treatment more extensive than Kant's and, as he lived in the gestation period of the new psychology, his influence on psychology in Germany was more direct and more fruitful. Wundt and his contemporaries who were preoccupied with psychology studied Herbart's two works relevant for psychology, the *Lehrbuch zur Psychologie* ("Textbook of Psychology," 1816), and the *Psychologie als Wissenschaft* ("Psychology as a Science," 1824-1825). Because of Herbart's prestige, anyone writing on psychology had to declare his stand with respect to the ideas expressed in these works. As there was support of Herbart's views, there was also opposition to them.

Psychology was defined by Herbart as a precise science, empirical, based not on physics or physiology, but on metaphysics and aided by mathematics. By these formulations Herbart furthered and strengthened psychology's scientific character. There were new psychological problems, thus far not discovered, to which Herbart called attention and whose study he foreshadowed such as those which in modern psychology come under the headings of the unconscious, attitude, and set. Some of his concepts, like the concept of apperception which he developed after Leibnitz, were to become quite important in the new psychology. Moreover, he extended the field of psychology, suggesting the study of different cultures, the mentally sick, animals, the utilization of observations and experiences of poets, artists, moralists, historians, and travellers. Some of these ideas were followed up and bore fruit in the achievements of his disciples. Herbart, who from his youth was interested in pedagogy and had personal teaching experience, demonstrated the need and value of psychology in education and called upon educators to use the findings of psychology. For this reason, he deserves the title of the originator of educational psychology.

On the negative side of Herbart's role in the new psychology is his exclusion of physiology and experimentation from psychology. He had no chance to appreciate their value and his philosophical bias was against them. The physiological and experimental aspect of psychology was better grasped by Hermann Lotze, Herbart's successor in the chair of philosophy at the University of Göttingen, a philosopher with a medical degree and a thorough training in physiology. After 24 years of teaching in Königsberg, Herbart accepted a professorship at Göttingen where he taught for eight years until his death in 1841. Three years later Lotze took his place and held this position for 37 years.

Hermann Lotze (1817-1881).

It happened that the two influential philosophers in the critical period of the emancipation of psychology, Herbart and Lotze, complemented each other in their contributions to psychology. Just as Herbart was a champion of the scientific character of psychology, so Lotze furthered the cause of experiment and physiology in psychology, giving a good example of keen observations and experimentation, and demonstrating their value for psychology. Whereas Herbart helped psychology in its theoretical aspect. Lotze enriched it with facts.

108

Although Lotze's philosophical views were valuable for philosophy and were well received by many, they were of no consequence for psychology and left no permanent trace in it, but the abundant facts and observations, and their interpretations in his writings, were of immediate significance for psychology. They were presented in such books as *Medicinische Psychologie oder Physiologie der Seele* ("Medical Psychology or the Physiology of the Soul," 1852), his most important work for psychology, and *Physiologische Untersuchungen* ("Physiological Investigations," 1853). Keenly interested in the explanation of space-perception like many of his contemporaries, he developed the hypothesis of "local signs." In this hypothesis he argued in favor of retinal areas and skin spots associated with certain visual or tactual sensations as being the most important factors in the perception of space. "Local sign" theory is still valid and is included in textbooks of psychology. It is obvious that such an explanation favors the empirical origin of both the concept and the perception of space and thus places Lotze in opposition to nativists who thought of space-perception as an innate datum of the mind.

The period of German psychology in which Lotze lived, so significant for the future of psychology, owes much to him as a spiritual parent and protector of many leading psychologists in Germany. From a historical point of view Lotze probably did more for psychology as a person and teacher than as a philosopher or writer. Among the disciples who came under his direct influence and whom he helped in various ways were Brentano, Stumpf, and G. E. Müller. The latter was his successor in Göttingen and director of its laboratory which was to become the second important center of psychological research and training after Leipzig. As a teacher, Lotze was inspiring and stimulating, and highly respected by his students. Külpe, one of the most important pioneers of psychology, writing about him, did not give Lotze much credit for his philosophy but said of him that he was "a source of inspiration" and "an excellent guide" to those who sought truth "honestly and profoundly."

Ernst Mach (1838-1916).

A philosopher and a physicist, a thinker and an experimentalist, Mach made many specific theoretical and experimental contributions to psychology. The country of his birth and activity was Austria, and the University of Prague, where he spent 28 years, the place of his greatest productivity. His experimental researches on vision, hearing, perception of rotation, of time, and of space, led him to many discoveries. Among other things he was able to explain the function of the semicircular canals of the inner ear and various phenomena of bodily rotation. His study of sensation brought out an early formulation of the concept of Gestalt. He demonstrated, for example, how two figures, identical geometrically, may not be psychologically identical.

The keen interest in sensation which Mach displayed was in harmony with his positivistic views. Positivism had in him its most ardent spokesman in Austria and Germany, and the most eloquent, too, for his writings were clear, convincing, and of excellent style. As a positivistic philosopher he was hostile to metaphysics, and so it is not surprising that he devoted to "anti-metaphysical prolegomena" the first section of his most important and most widely read book, *Analyse der Empfindungen* (1886, in English translation, "The Analysis of Sensations"). At the same time, also in the spirit of positivistic objectivity, he eagerly wanted psychology to be rigorously scientific. Mach's endeavors to make psychology less philosophical and more like other natural sciences, place him in the company of all whose efforts have effected a more quantitative and objectivistic psychology. No wonder that *Karl Pearson,* the founder of statistical techniques in psychology, was Mach's avowed admirer and follower. Those who worked toward this kind of psychology derived a great deal of inspiration from Mach. W. James respected Mach, visited him, and maintained contact with him for a long time. Writing of him he said: "I don't think any one ever gave me so strong an impression of pure intellectual genius." Philipp Frank, physicist and philosopher, professor of Harvard, who in his book *Modern Science and Its Philosophy* (1949) devoted two chapters to Mach, said of him that "he is still very much alive today." The "aliveness" is evident among other things in American Operationism which can claim Mach in its ancestry. Operationism developed from the ideas promulgated by the Vienna circle and Logical Positivism, and the real master of the Vienna circle, as Frank, one of its members stated, was no one else but Mach. Here we have another example of how a philosophy may be responsible for events which occur many years after its inception. History repeatedly shows that a philosopher or a writer often starts a chain reaction which long after his death may cause effects that were never envisaged by him.

Similar in views, but not as clear and convincing in their exposition, and not as influential for psychology as Mach, was his contemporary Swiss philosopher, *Richard Avenarius* (1843-1896). Both men recognized their philosophical affinity and mutual agreement in fundamental philosophical issues.

Herbert Spencer (1820-1903).

In England, the most influential figure in psychology after J. S. Mill, as we already know, was Bain; but second to him was H. Spencer. In his voluminous and numerous works Spencer endeavored to present all branches of knowledge and all the achievements of mankind. Biology, philosophy, sociology,

111

ethics, the history of public, social, and religious institutions—all were treated by him in separate volumes. The compendium devoted to psychology, *Principles of Psychology,* appeared as early as 1855. Neither a scientific genius nor an originator of any new philosophical system, Spencer nevertheless influenced psychology, largely by his evolutionary theory and its application to mental life. The latter was Spencer's truly original contribution. The philosophical orientation of his works followed both the Associationist tradition and Positivistic philosophy. As much as his philosophy is positivistic, however, it is not of the Comte brand. Spencer protested against being affiliated with the philosophy of the founder of Positivism with whom, according to his own testimony, he agreed only on methodology but differed on essential issues.

Evolution, a word which originated with Spencer, was his theme since 1852, seven years before Darwin's *Origin of Species.* The Spencerian theory of evolution embraced the whole universe in a continuous cosmic process of transformation from nebular condensation to the origin of life, to the beginning of mind, and to all the forms of social life in civilized nations. The most characteristic feature of Spencer's evolutionary theory is its extension to psychic life. Mind, and everything that we include in this word, is a product of the endless process of evolution. This process has no internal finality, it is a purely mechanical process which goes on, determined in its course inevitably by antecedents and chance circumstances. Since the mind, as we find it in man now, is a product of evolution, and its achievements are the result of the accumulation of all the experiences and events of the past, Spencer said, psychology should set out to study primitive men, animals, and go even to the lowest forms of animal life, to protozoa.

Genetic psychology in the United States stemmed from both Spencer's and Darwin's evolutionary theory. The psychologies of G. S. Hall and of J. M. Baldwin, the American builders of psychology, were inspired by this theory. Thorndike put Spencer's suggestion to practice when he began his experiments on animals. W. James, teaching evolution at Harvard, used Spencer's text, *First Principles* (1862), and he used his other texts as well. For his course in psychology, James adopted Spencer's *Principles of Psychology* and, despite violent opposition to Spencer's philosophical views, he kept it as a text for many years. A biographer of James, R. B. Perry, explains this rather odd fact by saying that Spencer "served James in the role of punching bag . . . in his intellectual gymnasium."

Positivism.

The school of Positivistic Philosophy or Positivism was founded by Auguste Comte (1798-1857), although early traces of this doctrine can be found in some writers of the eighteenth century. The positivistic system was presented in Comte's six-volume *Cours de philosophie positive* ("Course of Positive Philosophy," 1830-1842). Positivism was a violent reaction against existing philosophies. Particularly it rose against metaphysics, which in the hands of the extreme idealists was completely cut off from natural sciences, and against introspection as a scientific method and in the form which the French followers of the Scottish school advocated. The success of Positivism was considerable as most scientists of the nineteenth century rallied around it, and its effect continued into the twentieth century. A large part of Comte's writings was devoted to evolution, to the progress of mankind, and to various social phenomena. He is credited with stimulating social research and is regarded as the founder of scientific sociology.

Instrumental in spreading Comte's ideas in the Anglo-Saxon world, especially Comte's social views, were J. S. Mill, who publicly recognized his indebtedness to Comte, and Spencer, whom we have just discussed. Both of these English philosophers are regarded as representatives of Positivism despite their many important differences with Comte. E. Mach also followed Comte in many points but rejected his views on psychology. In general, positivistic philosophers differed in many respects from the founder of positivistic philosophy. Thus a distinction must always be made between the original positivistic philosophy of Comte and the doctrine of Positivism. The latter refers to the basic principles of positivistic philosophy and not necessarily to all its ramifications and applications as found in the writings of Comte.

Positivism and Psychology.

The fundamental tenet of Positivism is that the sensible comprises the whole sphere of knowledge and that anything that cannot be reached by the senses is unknowable. Consequently, Positivism radically rejected all metaphysics, that is, any inquiry aiming at finding the ultimate causes and the nature of things. The object of science is to discover facts, their relations and laws governing them.

With respect to psychology Comte showed a violent hostility. He denied that psychology, rational as well as empirical, was of any scientific value and he did not include psychology at all in his classification of sciences. "In no respect whatever," he stated, " is there any room for this illusory psychology, the final transmutation of theology, the revival of which is so vainly attempted today." The chief reason for this radicalism toward psychology was Comte's contempt for introspection as a scientific method. "Direct observation of the mind by itself is pure illusion," were his words. Only methods of natural sciences are valid, especially the method of induction. Hence, the data obtained through introspection are scientifically worthless. The use of introspection in psychology precludes, he said, any possibility of psychological studies of animals, children, and the mentally sick. All that psychology studied thus far, namely, mental phenomena and states of consciousness, belongs either to physiology because all mental phenomena can be reduced to cerebral functions or to history which can investigate the manifestations of the mind in time. That psychology can only be part of biology or physiology, was Comte's verdict.

Since Comte was determined to annihilate psychology as he understood it, one naturally cannot properly speak of any direct contribution by him to psychology. And yet Positivistic philosophy had a beneficial effect on psychology in a roundabout way by provoking a vigorous reaction in defense of psychology. It rallied psychologists, and compelled them to clarify the subject matter, methods, and aims of psychology. On the other hand, Positivistic philosophy initiated a strong striving for precision and objectivity in psychological inquiries, and this resulted in improvement of methods and procedures of psychology.

The country where positivistic philosophy had a strong hold on its rising psychology was Italy, mainly because of the powerful and enduring influence of Roberto Ardigo, professor at Padua University, who in 1870 published *La Psicologia come scienza positiva* ("Psychology as a Positive Science") in which he identified all mental life with cerebral physiology.

The positivistic undercurrent with its rejection of metaphysics and introspection, and its cry for objectivism, found its most complete expression in psychology in the school of Behaviorism and in so-called Behavioristics. Watson and other behaviorists may not have drawn their inspiration consciously or directly from Comte's writings but, nevertheless, it happened that metaphysics and introspection, which were the very reason for Comte's denial of scientific status to psychology, were banished by Behaviorism as the first step toward a new psychology, to be remade and remodelled after the natural sciences. As for social psychology, which was more directly influenced by Comte's philosophy, its concept of sociological determinism advocated by some psychologists is indeed a deliberate appropriation from Comte. It means that beliefs and attitudes of individuals or groups are the result of social and economic forces operating in a given society.

Henri Bergson (1859-1941).

As one of the most original philosophers of the modern era, and the most eminent in the last hundred years in France, Bergson gained wide recognition and captured the minds of many in Europe. His philosophy marks a vigorous reaction against materialism and narrow positivism. It was a resurrection of spiritualism garbed in fresh and attractive clothes.

It was like a dike put up against the swift current of mechanism, in Bergson's words, against the "mechanistic intoxication" of modern thought, which was spreading fast at the end of the nineteenth century. The effect of Bergson's ideas transcended the boundaries of philosophy and reached other fields of human thought, art, literature, ethics, and psychology. The books which contain a great deal of psychological material include: *Essai sur les données immédiates de la conscience* (1889), his first book, translated into English as *Time and Free Will: An Essay on the Immediate Data of Consciousness* (1913), *Matière et mémoire* ("Memory and Matter," 1896), *L'evolution créatrice* ("Creative Evolution," 1907), and partly *Le rire* ("Laughter," 1900). Psychological observations served Bergson as a foundation for his metaphysics.

Some characteristics of Bergsonian philosophy which have immediate implications for psychology are: 1) The existence of a universal living and creative impulse to continuous change and evolution. 2) The human mind is a dynamic unity. 3) The

116

emphasis on the unity of mind and on the ego as the substratum unifying the ever-changing psychological states. 4) The distrust of intellect in its ability to reach reality and the favoring of intuition as a better faculty. 5) Indeterminism. These characteristics put Bergson in opposition to the elementism of German psychology which he openly criticized. He also raised a voice of criticism against psychophysics directing his attack against the Belgian psychophysicist, Delboeuf. The stress on the unity of perceptual process made him a forerunner of the Gestalt school.

The effect of Bergson's philosophy was strong in France, and can be seen, for example, in the works of Dwelshauvers, C. Blondel, and in the psychiatry of Eugene Minkowski. The fact that France in general was cold toward German psychology and was tardy in instituting psychological experimentation can likely be traced, among other things, to Bergson's influence.

There is no noticeable influence of Bergson on American psychology, nor on English psychology. Bergson visited America and gave a series of lectures here. However, his first book, *Données immédiates,* very popular in France with 68 editions by 1948, was not translated into English until 25 years after its appearance (1913). But the initiator of American psychology, W. James, knew Bergson well. They met several times and remained good friends, and there was a real intellectual affinity between them. Their views in philosophy and psychology were similar and they both recognized this similarity. Both of them resisted atomistic psychology. The development of interest in religion which we find in James, had also occurred in Bergson, only it was stronger and more complete in the latter who in 1932, in his book *Les deux sources de la morale et la religion* ("Two Sources of Morality and Religion"), affirmed the spirituality and divinity of the ultimate reality. To conclude the evaluation of Bergson's role in psychology, we may note that

117

he was an enthusiastic spokesman for the spiritualistic concept of man which he sought to preserve and strengthen against mechanistic doctrines.

Neoscholasticism.

The term *Scholasticism* refers to the philosophical system of the Middle Ages. This system received its complete form in the works of Thomas Aquinas (1225-1274) who, as we have already mentioned, based his philosophy on Aristotle. Scholastic philosophy flourished in the thirteenth and fourteenth centuries. It began to decay in the fifteenth century, and in the sixteenth century it went into disrepute and was banished largely owing to the influence of the Cartesian philosophy which rejected Scholastic philosophy and partly to its lack of great talents capable of expounding and defending Aristotelian philosophy.

In the middle of the nineteenth century Scholastic philosophy, and particularly the philosophy of Thomas Aquinas, was revived under the name of Neoscholasticism or Neothomism. This revival received a strong impetus from Pope Leo XIII through his encyclical *Aeterni Patris* in 1879. The prefix *neo* in Neoscholasticism signified the fact that the followers of Scholastic philosophy set out to integrate this old philosophy with new attainments in the sphere of knowledge, giving heed to the Pope's admonition that "every wise thought and every useful discovery, wherever it may come from, should be gladly and gratefully welcomed." Neoscholastic psychology proceeded along the lines, for the most part, of Thomistic psychology, which we described before, integrating the old philosophical ideas with the findings of the new psychology and science in general, a characteristic henceforth common to all Neoscholastic psychologists. It attacked Cartesian dualism, and instead reiterated the hylomorphic doctrine. The pioneer of psychology who built on Thomism was Desiré Mercier (1851-1926) of Belgium, author of the two-volume *Psychologie* ("Psychology," 1892) and *Les Origines de la psychologie contemporaine* (translated into English as *The Origins of Contemporary Psychology,* 1897). The integration of the experimental and philosophical psychology in the spirit of Neoscholasticism was achieved by Joseph Fröbes, S. J. (1866-1947), well trained in both disciplines, and author of textbooks for them, the *Lehrbuch der experimentellen Psychologie* ("Textbook of Experimental Psychology", 1915-1920) which for a long time remained the best and largest source book for experimental psychology in the German language, and the *Psychologia speculativa* ("Speculative Psychology," 1927). Neoscholastic philosophy has served as a philosophical basis for the majority of Catholic psychologists. Although chiefly influential in Catholic circles, this philosophy was effective also in other provinces.

Aristotelian and Scholastic philosophies were already represented at some secular universities in the second half of the nineteenth century. A prominent spokesman for Aristotelian philosophy in Germany was F. A. Trendelenburg, professor of philosophy at Berlin University, whose student, Franz Brentano (1838-1917), through his writings made the influence of Aristotle felt in the new psychology. Brentano's place in the history of psychology is a prominent one inasmuch as, representing a different orientation from Wundt's, he became a source of inspiration for a large group of psychologists. He was a teacher of prominent men, among them Edmund Husserl and Sigmund Freud. There is no specific evidence, however, to indicate that Freud was influenced by his teacher.

Marxism.

The philosophy of Karl Marx (1818-1883), which was contemporary with the beginnings of experimental psychology—

119

his main work, *Capital,* appearing in 1867—had no effect on psychology at all at that time. Its contents could hardly have been expected to arouse the attention or interest of contemporary psychologists. But when Marxism became the official doctrine of Soviet Russia, psychology, along with other sciences, was subjugated by this doctrine and had to conform to the official teachings of Communism. Up to the Bolshevik revolution, in 1917, Russian psychology more or less followed the trends of the West, though with a strong physiological flavor; from 1917 on, however, it strode on a completely different path. It cut itself off entirely from the bourgeois West and developed along the Marxist principles. The effect of Marxism, in the interpretation of Lenin and other communistic writers of Soviet Russia, on that country's psychology is evident in the following characteristics: the materialistic concept of man and construction of psychology on materialistic principles, a strong emphasis on psychophysiology, and the treatment of psychological problems from the standpoint of the group, the society, rather than of the individual.

The materialism of Soviet psychology is different from the Western materialism which took shape in the second half of the nineteenth century. The latter is regarded as "naive" or "vulgar" by them, and that is why even such a system as Behaviorism could never completely satisfy the Russian psychologists, as indeed it did not. Dialectical materialism accepts "the ideal" along with "the material," and speaks of both the psyche and the body, but what is called "the ideal" (or "the psyche") is just the reflection of the material. Consciousness, too, is considered merely a product of the social being of men. One of the first to construct a system of psychology consistent with dialectical materialism was K. N. Kornilov in the mid-1920's. A considerable oscillation in the orientation of Russian psychology is evident afterwards, with ever-present conscious efforts to make it conform to the official doctrine of the leaders of the country.

The Sovietization of psychology resulted in a psychology which is limited, one-sided, sterile, and isolated. This psychology has been described by someone who has studied it and followed its development carefully as "dogma bound" and "straight-jacketed" (I. D. London).

National Differences in Philosophical Influences.

With respect to the effect of philosophy in different countries we must reiterate what we said earlier in this book (p. 35), namely, that this effect differed from country to country. Stronger in one nation, it was weaker in another. For example, while philosophy played a major role in the origin of psychology in Germany and Britain, it had a far less significant part in America. In the former countries, philosophical ancestry weighed heavily on psychology and the pioneers of psychology, particularly in Germany, were at the same time prominent philosophers. The founders of German psychology, like Wundt, Brentano, and Külpe were also first-rate philosophers and wrote philosophical books to the very end of their careers. Wundt, for instance, interspersed his psychological writings with voluminous works on logic, ethics, and metaphysics.

Psychology in America, on the other hand, was not preceded or molded by philosophers. Freshly imported as experimental psychology, it started without any philosophical ancestors or patrons. To be sure, before the appearance of experimental psychology, there was philosophical psychology in America (called mental philosophy), and also referred to as pre-Jamesian psychology, but the two psychologies, the old one and the new one, were entirely unrelated.

Going back to the case of Germany and Britain, even here, if one makes a comparison as to the respective strength of the

121

philosophical influence on the psychology of these countries, one must conclude that the philosophical ancestry was more important for German than it was for British psychology, the latter being also strongly affected by biology. In France, on the other hand, psychopathology predominantly shaped the character of psychology, philosophy playing only a secondary role in it. And so, in general, the effect and role of philosophy showed great variability among countries.

Moreover, there have also been national differences in the attitude toward present and future relations with philosophy. While in some countries we observe a tendency to keep psychology in close contact with philosophy and to maintain friendly relations with it, psychologists of other countries, considering philosophy as a restraining influence, a liability, have been hostile to any intercourse with philosophy and made every effort to keep the two apart. Germany belonged to countries of the former attitude, whereas the early psychology in the United States represented reactions of the latter type. Some remarks referring to this issue are to be noted in the conclusion at the end of the book.

When it comes to the effect of specific philosophical influences, of those which we have just discussed in this chapter as well as of the ones discussed previously, we can repeat that the effect of these systems was not the same in each country, indeed a particular system might have been altogether ineffective in some countries. Without going too far into the matter, we may cite some examples in order to illustrate the point in question. Evolutionism was particularly powerful in Britain and the United States, as evidenced in the general orientation of psychology, the educational psychology, and the success of comparative psychology. Positivism was the main root of the early Italian psychology; Herbart and Lotze prepared the ground for physiological psychology in Germany.

Bergsonism, without much effect on British or American psychology, made a marked impression on French psychology. Marxism was peculiar only to psychology in Soviet Russia.

SUMMARY

The aim of this chapter was to present the nineteenth century philosophical systems, which, in addition to Empiricism and Associationism, nourished psychology and shared in the responsibility for its original character and its subsequent development. Among them, the most notable were thought to be: the philosophy of Kant, the system of Herbart, the works of Lotze, the Positivism of Comte and Mach, the Evolutionism of Spencer, the views of Bergson, Neoscholasticism, and Marxism. Kantian philosophy tempered the effect of Empiricism and Associationism. Herbart and Lotze were the immediate preparation for psychology in Germany and were instrumental in psychology's emancipation and scientific status. Positivism brought psychology closer to the natural and physical sciences in theory and methods. Spencer introduced Evolutionism into psychology. Bergson tried to save psychology from materialism, while Neoscholastic philosophy insisted on the unity of man through the principle of a spiritual soul, and Marxism considered man as a materialistic reality molded by socio-economic forces. The effect of philosophy in general and specific philosophical systems on psychology differed from country to country. It was strong and lasting in some and weak and temporary in others.

SYNOPSIS OF
THE PHILOSOPHICAL ROOTS OF SCIENTIFIC PSYCHOLOGY

Philosophical Doctrines	Chief Representatives	Time
1. Dualism and the body-mind problem		
Solutions proposed:		
Hylomorphism	Aristotle	384-322 B.C.
Interactionism	Descartes	1596-1650
Parallelism	Leibnitz	1646-1716
Psychophysical parallelism	Bain	1818-1903
2. Empiricism	Hobbes	1588-1679
	Locke	1632-1704
	Berkeley	1685-1753
	Hume	1711-1776
3. Sensationism	Various philosophies particularly empiricism, associationism, and Scottish school	
4. Associationism	Hartley, founder	1705-1757
	Hume	1711-1776
	James Mill	1773-1836
	J. S. Mill	1806-1873
	T. Brown	1778-1820
	A. Bain	1818-1903
5. Various philosophies of the 19th century	Kant	1724-1804
	Herbart	1776-1841
	Lotze	1817-1881
	Mach	1838-1916
	Spencer	1820-1903
	19th c.	Positivism
	Bergson	1859-1941
	Neoscholasticism	since 1879
	Marxism	after 1920

INFLUENCE OF PHILOSOPHY ON PSYCHOLOGY

The influence of philosophy is evident in the *definition, character,* and *orientation* of the early psychology. This influence is particularly reflected in the following:

DEFINITIONS: Psychology is the study of immediate experience; study of consciousness and its states; science of the mind and its operations.

MAIN SUBJECT OF STUDY: Sensation and perception.

CHIEF METHOD: Introspection.

CHARACTERISTICS: Dualistic and elementistic.

Philosophical System		*Effect in Psychology*
Dualism	led to	Psychophysical parallelism
Empiricism	led to	Experimental character
Associationism	became	Philosophical foundation, resulted in making the process of association the key principle; elementism; search for physiological correlates of psychological processes; school of structuralism.
H. Spencer		Evolutionism
Positivism		Limitation or rejection of introspection; objectivity; quantification of psychological data; school of behaviorism.

Conclusion

Philosophy in its long history studied the nature of the world, God, and man. The philosophical study of the nature of man, his mind and mental operations, constituted a preparation for the scientific study of man's behavior, in other words, the philosophical ancestry of psychology which developed in the second half of the nineteenth century. The formulation of psychological problems and their solutions proposed by various philosophers, relevant concepts developed, all were phases of this ancestry. We have just surveyed them and called them the philosophical roots of scientific psychology.

Important Issues

Of the various issues of philosophy the most significant for psychology, historically speaking, we found, were: 1) the view that man was composed of two elements, a spiritual and a material, and the theories about the relationship between these two elements (the doctrine of dualism and the body-mind problem); 2) the inquiry into the source of man's knowledge, which led to the preoccupation with the study of sensation and perception; 3) the rejection of rationalism and rise of Empiricism; 4) process of association and theories about its function in mental operations developed by the school of Associationism. The latter doctrine gave psychology its basic theoretical foundation. Definition, subject matter, characteristics, and orientation of the new psychology were primarily the product of Associationism.

Emancipation from Philosophy.

The gradual development of psychological thought within

126

philosophy reached a point where the philosophical viewpoint and philosophical methods were found insufficient and a need for the scientific study of psychological problems was realized. Physiology played an important role in this realization. Development of scientific methods suited for psychology paved the way to its independence and progress. The result was that psychology claimed independence and broke away from philosophy. Emancipation of psychology became a reality and scientific psychology was born.

Relations with Philosophy.

After breaking away from philosophy in the second half of the nineteenth century and beginning its own independent existence, psychology could not, and did not, entirely sever its relations with philosophy. Philosophy continued to influence psychology. The residue of the various philosophical doctrines in psychology was often responsible for the latter's conflicts and difficulties. We may quote Wundt here, who said: "Psychology, even in our own day shows more clearly than any other experimental science traces of the conflict of philosophical systems. We may regret this influence in the interest of psychological investigation because it has been the chief obstacle in the way of an impartial examination of mental life. But in the light of history we see that it was inevitable." On the other hand, psychology itself also began in turn to influence philosophy.

The possibility of the collaboration between scientific psychology and philosophy has been recognized. This recognition was stronger in some psychologists and weaker or even absent in others. Different psychologists and different countries showed different attitudes towards the relations of psychology to philosophy.

In 1913, 107 professors of philosophy from universities of

Germany, Austria, and Switzerland issued a protest against the nomination of psychologists for the chairs of philosophy, arguing that such a practice was harmful to philosophy and that experimental psychology should have separate chairs. Reacting to this, Wundt in a special pamphlet, *Die Psychologie in Kampf ums Dasein* ("Psychology in the Struggle for its Existence," 1913), protested this move. He was strongly opposed to separate chairs of psychology because he felt that such a situation would create the danger of cutting psychology off completely from contact with philosophy, while psychology should be cultivated in close contact with philosophy. He appealed to the faculties of philosophy not to accept any candidate for *habilitation,* that is, an examination required in order to qualify for university professorship, who would only be an experimentalist and not also be well grounded in philosophy.

In 1905, at Harvard University, when a debate arose whether experimental psychology belongs within philosophy or within the natural sciences, H. Münsterberg, who was at that time in charge of the Harvard Psychological Laboratory, argued in favor of keeping psychology in philosophy. He referred to a letter received from Wundt who wrote to him: "I believe that psychology, not only now, but for all time, belongs to philosophy: only then can psychology keep its necessary independence."

Philosophy-Psychology Relationship Today.

Psychologists at the present time may differ in their opinions as to what the relationship between psychology and philosophy should be, but they all agree in the insistence on barring any bias of philosophical doctrines from the domain of psychological research. They seem to share the attitude of T. Lipps, the outstanding German psychologist and author of psychological textbooks, who said about himself: "Lecturing on psychology,

I am neither a materialist, nor an idealist, nor any other 'ist'—except a psychologist." On the other hand, they generally do not deny that turning to philosophy in the solution of theoretical problems is beneficial and even imperative for psychology and can only result in a better formulation of psychological theories, in a broader and deeper understanding of man who is the subject of psychology.

In recent years in America there has been, it seems, an ever increasing interest in what has been termed the "philosophy of psychology." The Minnesota Center for Philosophy of Science since its inception about eleven years ago has devoted most of its efforts towards the better understanding and formulations of the theoretical problems of psychology. The two volumes published by the Center in 1956 and 1958, respectively, the *Minnesota Studies in the Philosophy of Science,* testify to this fact. It is not surprising that many contemporary psychologists, even the most ardent experimentalists in America, belong to philosophical societies, participate in philosophical meetings, and write philosophical works. Several prominent members of the American Psychological Association are also active in the American Philosophical Society.

How its philosophical heritage still matters and reference to philosophy is still lively in the contemporary psychology, for example, in Great Britain, is reflected in a letter by W. Stephenson, a leader of present psychology in that country, published in the American Psychologist in 1948, from which we quote this characteristic fragment:

The great names of Hobbes, Locke, Hume, Berkeley, Hartley, the Mills, and Bain, and subsequently Galton, Pearson, Stout, and Spearman, still matter in England; and Scotland is just as proudly insinuative about its Reid, its Dugald Stewart, Brown, and Hamilton. The learned treatises from Britain, in recent decades, bear witness to these influences. In the case of Scotland, for example, perhaps the one imposing book of the past few decades is Drever's *Instinct*; and does it not breathe the very air of Dugald Stewart? And isn't it rumoured that Sir Cyril Burt sleeps with volumes of Mills under his pillow? In any case, his *Factors of the Mind,* Spearman's *Nature of Intelligence,* and Stout's *Analytical Psychology* are steeped deeply in the learning of these great historical names in psychology. Bartlett's *Remembering,* too, is redolent of the images and ghost of Berkeley. But something of this same historical nostalgia is felt throughout British psychology . . . . The philosophers in Britain, of course, won't let these great historical names rest; and, whatever the reason, psychology hasn't really broken with philosophy in Britain.

Suggested Readings

I.   Genealogy of psychology.

1.   There are several books on the *history of psychology*. Some give an account of the *entire* history, from the ancient times down to the modern era, while others present the history of scientific psychology with less extensive coverage of the philosophical foundation of psychology. To the former category belong:

Baldwin, J. M. *History of psychology*. London: Watts, 1913, 2 vols.
Brennan, R. E. *History of psychology from the standpoint of a Thomist*. New York: Macmillan, 1945.
Brett, G. S. *A history of psychology*. London: Allen & Unwin, 1912, 1921, 3 vols.
Brett, G. S. *A history of psychology*. (Edited and abridged by R. S. Peters) . New York: Macmillan, 1953.
Brett, G. S. *Psychology, ancient and modern*. New York: Longmans, 1928.
Spearman, C. E. *Psychology down the ages*. London: Macmillan, 1937, 2 vols.

Books concerned with the history of *scientific* psychology are:

Boring, E. G. *A history of experimental psychology*. 2nd. ed. New York: Appleton-Century-Crofts, 1950.
Flugel, J. C. *A hundred years of psychology,* 2nd ed. London: Duckworth, 1951.
Heidbreder, E. *Seven psychologies*. New York: Appleton-Century-Crofts, 1933.
Klemm, O. *History of psychology*. New York: Scribner, 1914.
Müller-Freienfels, R. *The evolution of modern psychology*. New Haven, Conn.: Yale Univer. Press, 1935.
Murchison, C. (Ed.) *A history of psychology in autobiography*. Worcester, Mass.: Clark Univer. Press, 1930-1936. 3 vols.
Volume 4 of the same series was edited by Langfeld, Boring, Werner, and Yerkes; it appeared in 1952.
Murchison, C. (Ed.) *The psychological register*. Worcester, Mass.: Clark Univer. Press, 1929-1932. 3 vols.

Murphy, G. *Historical introduction to modern psychology*. Rev. ed. New York: Harcourt, Brace, 1949.

Pillsbury, W. B. *The history of psychology*. New York: Norton, 1929.

Villa, G. *Contemporary psychology*. New York: Macmillan, 1903.

Of these, the most comprehensive, up-to-date, and recognized as the classic in the field is: Boring, E. G., *A history of experimental psychology*. 2nd ed., 1950. This book is a good source of further references. It should be consulted first when references related to topics covered in our book are desired.

Excerpts from original works relevant to the history of psychology have been collected in:

Dennis, W. *Readings in the history of psychology*. New York: Appleton-Century-Crofts, 1948.

Rand, B. *The classical psychologists*. New York: Houghton Mifflin, 1912.

2. The student desirous of more detailed information on the *philosophical systems* should consult standard textbooks of history of philosophy or monographs dealing with various systems or historical periods. These textbooks usually contain bibliographies arranged according to subject which will help the student in the selection of further reading.

Bochenski, I. M. *Contemporary European philosophy*. Translated by D. Nicholl and K. Aschenbrenner from the 2nd rev. German ed. Berkeley and Los Angeles: Univ. of Cal. Press, 1956.

Collins, J. D. *A history of modern European philosophy*. Milwaukee: Bruce, 1954.

Copleston, F. C. *A history of philosophy*. Westminster, Md.: Newman Press, 1946-60. 6 vols.

Fuller, B. A. *A history of philosophy*. 3rd ed. Rev. by S. M. Mc Murrin. New York: Holt, 1955.

Gilson, E. H. *History of Christian philosophy in the Middle Ages*. New York: Random House, 1955.

Muelder, W. G. and Sears, L. *The development of American philosophy.* Boston: Houghton Mifflin. New edition, 1960.
Owens, J. *A history of ancient Western philosophy.* New York: Appleton-Century-Crofts, 1959.

There are also books which compile characteristic passages from significant philosophical works. An example of this kinds is:

Runes, D. D. *Treasury of philosophy.* New York: Philosophical Library, 1955.

But there are many others, general and specialized. Very helpful for general information on philosophical concepts and doctrines, as well as for bibliography, will be:

Baldwin, J. M. *Dictionary of philosophy and psychology.* New York: Macmillan, 1902, 1905. New edition, 1928. 3 vols.

Recommended for their treatment of the philosophical foundation of psychology are:

Barbado, M. *Introduction à la psychologie expérimentale.* Paris: Lethielleux, 1931. Translated from the Spanish.
Mercier, D. *The origins of contemporary psychology.* London: Washbourne, 1918.
Ribot, T. A. *English psychology.* New York: Appleton-Century-Crofts, 1874.
Ribot, T. A. *German psychology of today.* New York: Scribner's, 1886.
The last three books are translations from the French.

II. Psychology within philosophy

On Descartes: Wallon, H. La psychologie de Descartes.
Pensée, 1950, *32,* 11-20.
Balz, A. G. A. (Ed.) *Cartesian studies.* New York: Columbia Univer. Press, 1951.

On Vives: Watson, F. The father of modern psychology.
Psychol. Rev., 1915, *22,* 333-353.

III. Dualism and the body-mind problem

General studies:

Feigl, H. The "Mental" and the "Physical." In *Minnesota Studies in the Philosophy of Science*. Minneapolis: Univ. of Minnesota Press, 1958. Vol. II, pp. 370-497.

McDougall, W. *Body and mind*. New York: Macmillan, 1911.

Reeves, Joan W. *Body and mind in Western thought*. Baltimore: Penguin, 1958.

Weber, C. O. Theoretical and experimental difficulties of modern psychology with the body-mind problem. In P. L. Harriman (Ed.) *Twentieth century psychology*. New York: Philosophical Library, 1946.

On the hylomorphic doctrine of Aristotle there is an excellent study:

Siwek, P. *La psychophysique humaine d'après Aristote*. Paris: Alcan, 1930.

On the Cartesian doctrine in physiology:

Pirenne, M. H. Descartes and the body-mind problem in physiology. *Brit. J. Phil. Sci.,* 1950, *1,* 43-59.

With reference to the section *The first attempt at experimental psychology,* see:

Mintz, A. An eighteenth century attempt at an experimental psychology. *J. gen. Psychol.,* 1954, *50,* 63-77.

For chapter V read:

Boring, E. G. *Sensation and perception in the history of psychology*. New York: Appleton-Century-Crofts, 1942.

For chapter VI:

    Warren, H. C. *A history of association psychology*. New York: Scribner, 1921.

For Conclusion:

    Feigl, H. Philosophical embarrassments of psychology. *Amer. Psychologist*, 1959, *14*, 115-128.

Index